GV
854.85   Foss, Merle L.
F67
         Ski conditioning

40123 -2

DATE DUE			
NOV 14 '79	DEC 1 3 '93		
JAN 14 '80			
FEB 25 '81			
OCT 19 '81			
DEC 15 '81			
MAR 1 0 1983			
APR 8 1983			
OCT 3 1984			

SKI CONDITIONING

AMERICAN COLLEGE OF SPORTS MEDICINE SERIES

SKI CONDITIONING
Merle L. Foss and James G. Garrick

**CONDITIONING FOR DISTANCE RUNNING:
THE SCIENTIFIC ASPECTS**
Jack Daniels, Robert Fitts, and George Sheehan

THE PHYSIOLOGY AND BIOMECHANICS OF CYCLING
Irvin Faria and Peter Cavanaugh

**HEALTH AND FITNESS
THROUGH PHYSICAL ACTIVITY**
Michael Pollock, Jack Wilmore, and Samuel Fox

SKI
CONDITIONING

MERLE L. FOSS
University of Michigan

JAMES G. GARRICK
University of Washington

JOHN WILEY & SONS
New York   Santa Barbara   Chichester   Brisbane   Toronto

Library of Congress Cataloging in Publication Data:

Foss, Merle L., 1936–
    Ski conditioning.

    (American College of Sports Medicine series)
    Bibliography: p.
    Includes index.
    1. Skis and skiing–Training. 2. Exercise.
I. Garrick, James G., joint author. II. Title. III. Series

GV854.85.F67   796.9'3   77-24553
ISBN 0-471-26764-3

Printed in the United States of America

10 9 8 7 6 5 4 3 2 1

About The Authors

Merle L. Foss, Ph.D. FACSM, Associate Professor of Physical Education and Director of Physical Performance Research Laboratory. The University of Michigan.

James G. Garrick, M.D., FACSM, Head, Division of Sports Medicine, Associate Professor, Department of Orthopedic Surgery, University of Washington, Seattle.

FOREWORD

During the past 10 years, a tremendous explosion of knowledge has occurred in the exercise and sport sciences. New theories in the coaching and training of athletes have emerged, technological breakthroughs have allowed a better understanding of how people perform and adapt to the stress of exercise, and we now have a better understanding as to how exercise can improve both the quality and quantity of life. In addition, the population of the United States has become more conscious of physical fitness and has started exercising on their own, with little or no knowledge of what to do or how to go about it. Consequently, many commercial enterprises have evolved to satisfy this basic consumer need. Although many of these enterprises have provided valuable consumer services, there are many others that have not had the consumer's best interests at heart and have taken advantage of the general lack of knowledge of the average consumer.

In 1973, the American College of Sports Medicine, at the suggestion of their former President, Dr. Howard G. Knuttgen, planned a series of volumes to help bridge the widening gap between the latest research in the exercise and sport sciences and the consumer. The purpose of this Series was to bring to the level of the average consumer, the facts and basic information related to exercise in general, and individual sports specifically, in an interesting and unbiased manner. Dr. David L. Costill, currently President of the American College of Sports Medicine, was asked to initiate this Series.

The American College of Sports Medicine's Series is an exciting step forward in the area of consumer education. Each volume is co-authored by authorities in their respective areas, who were selected for their ability to communicate their ideas at a very practical and fundamental level. While each of these authors is a recognized scientist, each volume represents an attempt to apply the teachings and findings of science to the better understanding of and participation in various activities and sports. It is the intent of this Series to develop a more informed consumer and to stimulate widespread participation in a variety of activities and sports.

JACK H. WILMORE
Chairperson, Publications Committee
American College of Sports Medicine

ACKNOWLEDGEMENTS

Appreciation is expressed to the following who contributed in a variety of ways during preparation of this monograph:

Richard Bowers, Ph.D., FACSM, Bowling Green University, Bowling Green, Ohio

Margaret Collins, Student Member ACSM, The University of Michigan, Ann Arbor, Michigan

Donald Hook, Student Member ACSM, The University of Michigan, Ann Arbor, Michigan

Richard Lampman, Ph.D., Member ACSM, The University of Michigan, Ann Arbor, Michigan

Thomas Ludwig, Director of Mt. Holly Ski Patrol, Mt. Holly, Michigan

Roger Passmore, Member ACSM, Wilfrid Laurier University, Waterloo, Ontario, Canada

Richard Redfearn, Ph.D., FACSM, Michigan State University, East Lansing, Michigan

Ralph Requa, Member ACSM, University of Washington, Seattle

M.F.
J.G.G.

CONTENTS

Contents

SECTION 1
Introduction

"To *play* at a sport is one thing, to *compete* in the same sport is quite a different matter," say many professional athletes in later years, as they feel their youthful vigor waning and consider ending their careers. The implication is that, although they can still play and enjoy most aspects of the sport, competition requires a training commitment that exceeds their level of motivation or a level of training that is impossible because of injuries or aging effects. Although the above statement applies to skiing, the vast majority of skiers pursue the sport, as is done in other forms of athletics, on a recreational and enjoyment basis instead of as an outlet for competitive drives or professional monetary gain. The major aim of this book, therefore, is to increase the enjoyment of recreational skiers.

How do you reasonably proceed to increase a participant's level of enjoyment? What do you provide to increase a participants enjoyment? Our plan gives a unique description of the sport of skiing in terms of equipment, injury occurrence and recognition, and associated medical problems as well as a description of muscular, physiological, and neuropsychological needs. This section, which includes scientific documentation whenever possible will contribute to the reader's enjoyment of skiing by more acutely sensitizing them to their own safety

1

needs and the hazards of being inadequately "equipped," whether in terms of apparatus, knowledge, or physical conditioning. Our premise is that noninjured skiers enjoy their sport more.

The sections on the muscular, physiological, and neuropsychological considerations of Section 4 are the foundation for subsequent chapters. The major objective is to improve the scientific approach to training and conditioning by first identifying the basic ingredients of the sport of skiing and then progressing to considerations of optimum training to enhance these ingredients. This procedure eliminates much of the random, "shotgun" approach to training that has been evident in many previous manuals on ski conditioning. The reader will readily observe that Section 4 does not contain a section on ski technique. This exclusion is by design, since we feel that ski technique, as much as it can be appreciated through printed material, has been covered well in other books (1-3) and periodic publications (4, 5). Our purpose is to increase the enjoyment of skiers by increasing the knowledge base on which they operate, since it is well known that appreciation for detail and enjoyment of activities are closely related, that is, the more you enjoy, the more you wish to know, knowing more increases enjoyment and the like. If nothing else, it creates more lively discussions and arguments about the best way to train for sports and stimulates more inquiry into the WHY for doing something in a particular way. Such inquiry usually leads the thinking consumer to question whether recommended training techniques have any scientific basis of support and to discover that they are frequently only based on expert opinion and "hand-me-down" coaching dictates. Since these queries are coupled to initiation of better training programs or modification of existing programs, we feel the criterion of contributing to the skiers' enjoyment will once again be met.

A third way in which this text contributes to skier enjoyment is through a direct improvement in technical skill and skiing ability. Although mentioned last, a statement like, "I'm skiing better now" summarizes the interwoven nature of previously mentioned considerations such as reductions in ski injuries, avoidance of hazards, proper equipment selection, enlarged knowledge base, and improved physical condition. The exact reason why a person is skiing better becomes a matter of only academic interest—the primary matter is that progress has been made, and the skier realizes it. The acquisition of some new skills will be the strongest motivation for the skier to practice new techniques, to overcome the psychological barrier of an "impossible" slope (whether it be intermediate, expert, or truly impossible), or to simply desire to ski more. In Sections 6 and 7, we describe conditioning and warm-up programs that should reasonably prepare the skier in advance so that more slope-time can be spent concentrating on technique and skill acquisition. Section 8 is included as an aid to National Ski Patrol members and instructors who are requested to conduct ski conditioning and training workshops in a variety of settings. Figure 1 summarizes the major ways in which the material of this book contributes to skier enjoyment.

1. Extend years of participation.
2. Increase knowledge base.
3. Reduce injury rates.
4. Increase level of skill and conditioning.
5. "Sensitize" to hazards.
6. Optimize training techniques for improving skill or conditioning.
7. Question and teach the "why" of training drills.

FIGURE 1. Possible ways to improve skier enjoyment.

SECTION 2
Description of the Sport

GENERAL DESCRIPTION

Skiing is almost unique among sports. Prerequisites for skiing − except the requirement for snow − are nearly nonexistent, and because of this situation, the potential for medical and safety problems is great.

All things considered, skiing can be a reasonably safe activity − even with no preparation. Each year, more people die while watching football games than do while skiing. Indeed, deaths or even severely disabling injuries attributable only to skiing (and not previously existing cardiorespiratory problems) are exceedingly uncommon.

When we consider skiing in an athletic context, it is difficult to explain how safe it actually is. Average skiers are reasonably sedentary or, at best, intermittently active people in their mid-twenties, who leave early in the morning for the ski area. After two to three hours in the fetal position in the car, they encase their feet, ankles, and lower legs in form-fitting plastic boots, effectively immobilizing that part of their anatomy better than the best orthopedic surgeons.

To these boots they affix steel or fiberglass lever arms that measure from three to seven feet in length. Then, without warm-up or stretching − except the walk to the tow − they sit on a chairlift completely exposed to the elements for 5 to 25 minutes. Descending from the lift, they face a one-quarter to three-mile trip down terrain which, although familiar, will be covered with snow of any description.

Even with this almost reckless disregard for all of the precepts of traditional athletic activities, for example, conditioning, warm-up and coaching to achieve expertise, the skier seems blessed by Ullr,* since the overall likelihood of injury is only 1 in 100 per outing. Still, a 14-percent chance of injury during the course of the entire ski season could be improved upon. With proper preparation, skiing can be safer. If increased safety is not attained, preparation, at least, can make skiing more enjoyable.

One of the problems of dealing with skiing from a safety — or even enjoyment — standpoint is that nearly everyone is a potential skier. Children start skiing as soon as they are able to walk, and octogenarians are common on the slopes. Sex barriers in skiing are virtually nonexistent and have been for decades. Even physical handicaps do not preclude skiing in many instances. Indeed, the desire to ski by those with specific medical conditions — the blind or the amputee — has resulted in the establishment of special training courses for them.

The almost universal opportunity to ski, while democratic, is a mixed blessing. Few if any other sports, with the same potential for injury as skiing, exist with as few controls. Once the ski lifts are operating, almost every skier can attempt every slope under every weather and snow condition. Predictably, problems arise.

It is not our intention to write a book on ski injuries, but injuries are and always have been a part of skiing. Actually, the risk of injury may make skiing appealing to some. Injuries surely do determine the amount of pleasure obtained from the sport. Thus the injuries and their relationship to equipment, abilities, conditioning, and experiences, for example, will be presented here with the hope that a better informed skiing population will ski more safely.

EQUIPMENT

Skier safety and enjoyment rely more heavily on equipment than almost any other sport except organized football. Ski equipment has two useful purposes: proper execution of the maneuvers required by the sport and protection of the wearer.

*The Norse god of skiing.

Execution/expertise and its relationship to equipment is as individual as a fingerprint, and only the individual can decide what items will best transform him or her into a graceful, controlled, and accomplished skier. What works for the Olympic gold medal winner in the slalom may not be appropriate for the weekend skier who is barely able to negotiate lift ramps without falling. Generally, equipment used by experts is designed for experts. Beginners and intermediates should obtain the equipment designed for them since, often, it will enable them to perform to the limits of their capabilities.

BOOTS. The skier's first and probably most significant purchase is boots. To allow and encourage proper execution of maneuvers, the boot must be "part of the skier." Anything that is going to conform to every muscle, bone, and tendon must be chosen with care. The "mild discomfort" in the ski shop is the blister or "bone bruise" after a day's skiing. Boots must fit and fit confortably. All ski boots — even well-fitting ones — feel abnormal because we're used to having movement at our ankles as well as in the small joints in our feet. If these movements are eliminated, walking becomes a loping, rolling gait — different and even awkward, but not painful. After all, ski boots were made for skiing, not walking. If more concessions are made to allow for comfortable walking, edge transfer and other motions of skiing will be less precise. The less motion present at the ankle, the more direct will be the transfer of knee motion to the skis — necessary for performing the techniques taught today.

Actually, few ski boots block all ankle motion. Even though the shell of the boot might seem as rigid as sheet metal, the foam or other materials used to achieve the fit is compressible. Therefore, even if the boot is rigid and has a locked hinge — or no hinge at all — by leaning forward, some ankle motion is possible by compressing the padding in the front or back of the boot. In addition, in most boots, the foot slides forward and backward with attempted ankle motion. This is one of the sources of boot-related injury problems in skiing.

Repeatedly leaning forward in most boots results in complete compression of the padding at the top of the front of the boot. No matter how soft or resiliant the padding feels, once it is maximally compressed it becomes as hard as the substance underlying it — in this case, the front, top edge of the shell. Because the front of the leg/shin is poorly padded, there is repeated trauma to the front of the tibia — the large bone in the lower leg, located directly beneath the skin in the front. The resulting "bone bruises" can be as painfully disabling as a sprained ankle or knee.

This problem can be prevented by a boot hinged in such a manner that the entire front of the boot tilts to maintain a parallel relationship with the front of the leg, thus distributing the pressure over a large area − the entire front of the boot. Unfortunately, since few boots are so designed, it is up to the skier to pad the shin. Attempting to protect an area from pressure is a matter of redistributing the pressure, usually either over a larger area or to an area better able to accept the pressure (e.g., muscle rather than bone). This redistribution is best accomplished by a donut or "U-shaped" pad with the center located over the tender area. This results in distributing the force around the problem area. Such pads can be made from the readily available semirigid foams. The stiff, upper edge of the boot shell on the outside can cause this part of the boot to indent the lateral (outside) portion of the leg − often resulting in bruises and, frequently, in fractures of the fibula. Use of a "donut-shaped" pad may also help in this area.

Currently available ski boots, because of their fit and rigidity, may protect the ankle at the expense of some other structure. With increased usage of high, rigid, well-fitting ski boots, the frequency of ankle injuries (sprains and fractures) appears to have decreased. Unfortunately, there has been a comparable increase in fractures of the tibia or fibula (lower leg) and at least a suggestion of increasing frequencies of knee sprains as well.

From a performance standpoint, ski boot design may also play a role in ski safety. Generally, the more proficient skier skis more safely. Part of increased proficiency is the ability to properly use the ski edges. Edging, then, is partly a function of boot fit and rigidity. If the boot is designed so that the skier's weight is transmitted more to the inside or outside edges of the skis, some modicum of ski control will be lost. Partially because this problem does exist with some boots, a leveling device was designed to equally distribute the skier's weight on the ski edges. Although ski "canting" − as this leveling process is called − can be used to help skiers with bowlegs or knock-knees to ski with better edge control, as often as not, the wedge (or cant) placed between boot and ski merely compensates for the lack of anatomic design of many boots. A simplistic explanation is that, although the leg (above the ankle) is not a cylinder but rather an asymmetrical truncated cone, it is forced into a generally cylindrical receptacle, the upper part of the boot. Because the leg is also asymmetrical, placing it into a cylindrical receptacle causes it to enter the boot at an angle, thereby influencing the amount of weight borne on the inside or outside of the foot and making proper edging more difficult.

Anatomically designed ski boots do not seem to have this problem and will require canting less frequently. Thus, if skiers plan on their weight being distributed on their skis, as it is on the floor when they stand barefoot, the silhouette of the ski boot (from the back) should resemble that of their leg viewed from the same position. Remember, ski boots are performance items of equipment. They are designed to permit the rapid and accurate transfer of forces from the skier to the ski in a painless manner. If they fail at these tasks, they are not good boots. They are not primarily items of safety equipment.

SKIS. Although boots and bindings should probably be the skier's priority purchase, skis are usually viewed as most important. Skis come in an infinite combination of lengths, widths, flexes, cambers, side cuts, and materials. Because of their durability, they can be a long-term investment and, during the years of use, are almost maintenance-free. As with boots and ski clothing, ski styles change almost yearly.

Skis, like boots, are primarily performance items of equipment. One might argue that the "right" skis encourage more proficient — and safer — skiing. True — but they are still primarily performance items of equipment. Most skis are designed with specific purposes in mind. The ski designed for the deep, dry, powder snow of Colorado will be less than effective on blue ice and vice versa. Also, the ski used by world-class racers to win slalom events may not be appropriate for a Sunday afternoon on the intermediate slopes. If asked, the honest and concerned ski-shop owners can match the skiers (height, weight, abilities, etc.) with the proper skis. Because they are in business, they will sell you any ski you demand.

Ski length is probably important in ski safety because shorter skis result in less rotational force applied to the legs and knee, in the event of a fall. Although not thoroughly documented, there appears to be some decrease in the frequency of skiing injuries coincident with the increased popularity of shorter skis. Ski length may also play another more subjective role in ski safety. Shorter skis are easier to turn and were initially developed to aid in teaching novices. The graduated-length methods (GLM) of instruction also initially employ shorter skis — lengthening the skis as skiers increase their expertise.

It has been suggested that the use of the GLM might influence safety in several ways. Some feel that skiing is "too easy" on the short skis and that skiers advance in their ability to accomplish turn maneuvers too fast for their experience. Thus, it might be possible to execute expert maneuvers (and thus ski expert terrain) before one has the experience to deal with varying snow conditions, narrow trails, crowded slopes, and the like. Surely experience plays a role in ski safety, but the experience that results in low-injury rates is probably measured in years rather than the days involved in GLM teaching. On the positive side, shorter skis may be safer skis simply because they are easier to control. Generally, avoiding falls means avoiding injuries, and the more easily skiers are able to control their skis, the less likely they are to fall. Aside from the safety considerations, shorter skis have positively affected the sport by allowing thousands of beginning and intermediate skiers to maneuver more easily and confidently.

A potential nonskiing safety problem has arisen with the popularity of shorter skis — the hazard they present inside an automobile. In the past, it was difficult, at best, to carry one's skis in the car. Recently, many skiers have foregone the expense of a cartop ski rack and placed the skis across the seats. In the event of a panic stop or collision, the potential for injury from flying, sharp skis should be recognized and heeded.

SKI POLES. Poles are primarily performance items of equipment with two possible exceptions — the tips and the straps. There is little to remember about the tips, except that they are sharp, and can result in lacerations and puncture wounds.

Pole straps allow one to plant the pole harder by pulling down on the strap; thus the pole need not be gripped as tightly. This can be accomplished by merely putting the hand through the loop rather than securing it around the wrist. The latter practice can result in two mechanisms of injury. If the basket gets caught (in a tree or fence or in the snow), the arm can be carried out and backward resulting in shoulder injuries — not uncommon for skiers. Hand injuries, often fractures, are the second problem. These injuries are the result of trying to break one's fall with a hand still gripping the pole. With the strap wrapped around the wrist, it is difficult to discard the pole — a proper maneuver when falling.

A dropped ski pole is of little consequence. Unlike a lost ski, it is unlikely to injure anyone and can be retrieved easily, since (1) it won't go very far, and (2) one can ski without it.

BINDINGS. Bindings have a twofold purpose, which seems enigmatic: they hold skiers on the ski and let them loose. The binding capable of simultaneously serving these performance and safety functions has not been made and, therefore, skiers should know as much as possible about the device to which they entrust the health of their lower extremities.

Only two decades ago, bindings served a single purpose: to attach skiers — by means of their boots — to the ski. A binding incapable of release sounds, today, like an invitation to disaster, but the ski-binding-boot-skier system was not always as rigid as it is today. Skis were wooden and, occasionally, when the system was stressed, the ski broke rather than the skier. Boots were leather and were known to release the skier, even though they were still attached to the binding. Boot soles were leather, softened with time, and they were often flexible enough to make retention in the binding difficult — a safety function of sorts.

As boots became stiffer and better fitting, skis metal and more durable, and skiers more demanding of precise ski (edge) control, the need for escape became more critical, and bindings were designed to release as well as to retain. Touted as "safety bindings," their performance fell short of this laudable goal. The next development was the "step-in" binding — almost universally used today. Although the transition from nonrelease to cable-type bindings was unaccompanied by any appreciable increase in ski safety, the move to step-in bindings resulted in a documentable, albeit modest, decrease in ski injury rates.

Obviously someone — ski industry or skiing public — felt that step-in bindings were still inadequate from a safety standpoint, since there followed the development and sales of a number of devices allowing the skier to "properly adjust" those step-in bindings. Although almost universally embraced by the ski industry and publications, use of the settings suggested on the testing devices has resulted in no demonstrable reduction in the occurrence of ski injuries.

Binding testing devices do, however, allow skiers to find out if their bindings will release at all. Thus even if one ignores the tables of suggested settings, the testing devices can serve an important function. Not surprisingly, an appreciable number of bindings, either as a result of improper installation or maintenance, will not release. Discovering this fact in the ski shop is less hazardous than finding out in the midst of a fall.

The final development was that of antifriction devices (AFD's). These low-friction pads are interposed between ski and boot sole and, in their simplest form — the teflon pad — appear to offer an added degree of protection. No such evidence is currently available with regard to the mechanical AFD's. Remember, however, that AFD's are designed to assist in the prevention of very specific injuries — that is, those resulting from a fall while still bearing weight on the ski. Because this mechanism occurs infrequently, the efficacy of AFD's will be difficult to document.

There appears to be little documentation on a "safe" binding. Indeed, the major brands appear to offer more or less the same degree of protection. Even if a binding were shown to be "safe," that is, release when necessary, skiing injuries would not disappear. Injuries can be — and are — sustained even if skiers are freed from their skis. Hand and wrist fractures, shoulder dislocations, and concussions are all common injuries suffered by skiers and have little to do with the ski remaining attached to a skier's foot. Indeed, the capability of release allows occasional premature releases that can result in injury.

How then might skiers insure that they receive the maximum protection available from their equipment? Whatever protection might be afforded by one's equipment is negated if the various devices do not work as they are designed to. Thus the bindings must move, as designed, to allow release. The pragmatic test is to stand on the skis and be able to painlessly twist out of the bindings. This will be difficult, if not impossible, if the binding is rusted, filled with road grit or salt, bent or otherwise damaged, or improperly mounted. There is no test device that has proved to be more reliable than this pragmatic, prosaic, and inexpensive test. It should be performed at least every day at the onset of skiing.

CLOTHING. There are few circumstances in sports where the participant has as many options in choosing a "uniform" as in skiing. Seemingly, ski clothing must only preserve enough modesty to prevent arrest and enough body heat to prevent hypothermia. Actually, the skier's uniform should serve a number of protective/safety functions.

Ski clothing should provide adequate warmth; for example, it should preserve body heat. How much body heat you need to preserve depends on where you ski. Subzero weather requires layers (long underwear, etc.) and often down-filled or other air-entrapping outer-wear. The ultimate in cold weather clothing is usually not "chic." If looking slim is important, then either ski in warmer climates or prepare to be cold. Ski clothing should protect against the elements (other than cold). The two most distressing natural elements — except cold — are wind and sunlight. Tightly woven/knitted outer garments or shells protect against the former; any garment protects against the latter.

Sunlight is a real hazard to the skier. The ultraviolet, sunburn-producing portion of sunlight operates maximally at ski areas. Ski areas are often at high altitudes in pollution-free areas. Thus, there is less atmosphere to screen out the ultraviolet rays, In addition, snow is an almost perfect reflector of ultraviolet rays. Shorts and a T-shirt (or less) may seem a good way to get an edge on the summer's tan during sunny, spring skiing. However, many ski vacations have been halted by a sunburn that is too painful to allow wearing clothing, much less skiing. Sunburns requiring hospitalization are not uncom-mon.

The other "element" against which skiers must protect themselves is their equipment. Ski edges, bindings, and boot buckles all have sharp edges or surfaces; and, although most lacerations that occur during skiing are insignificant, they can spoil a day's skiing and can partially be prevented by ski pants and long underwear.

Finally, ski clothing should not cause injuries. The shiny, wet-look fabrics have no place on the ski slope — indeed, they have been out-lawed in some instances. Since they not only look slippery but are slippery, the friction between skier and snow, necessary to stop one after a fall, is appreciably decreased. Deaths have been reported as a result of falls on steep, icy, or packed slopes with the skier continuing to slide until stopped by some obstacle. If these fabrics are to be used, bands of a more abrasive material should be sewed to the surface.

When choosing gloves, socks, and other accessories one should remember that warmth requires circulating blood, and constricting bands around wrists and ankles are not only uncomfortable but lead to cold hands and feet. Glove cuffs need only be tight enough to keep the snow out.

SECTION 3
Ski Injuries: To Whom and Why?

Ski injuries probably receive more public attention than the medical problems associated with any other recreational activity. Part of the perceived danger of the sport is therefore artifactual and results from an occasional, prominent individual being injured and receiving untoward attention from the news media. Another reason that skiing is perceived as inherently dangerous is because practically every cartoon of skiers or skiing deals with injuries or accidents.

Most skiers like to perpetuate the aura of danger surrounding the sport — indeed, ski injuries are worn as merit badges or service stripes. Ski shops sell brilliantly colored socks to wear over leg casts. Pins to be worn on parka or jacket depict crossed crutches to designate the wearer as a survivor of the rigors of the sport.

Obviously, there must be some element of truth to this readily accepted and prevalent "myth." Skiing does indeed carry with it an appreciable risk of injury. To say, however, that skiing is more (or less) dangerous than any other sport or recreational activity is difficult if not impossible. Since there are few other recreational activities that involve as diverse a population as skiing, most comparisons are meaningless.

Skiing injuries are noteworthy only because they occur as seldom as they do. Consider, for instance, participants whose ages span eight decades; involvement of both sexes; a general lack of physical conditioning (because the participants are a cross section of the general population who are poorly conditioned); a hostile environment that requires increased energy just to stay warm much less be active; less oxygen in the air than most are accustomed to; sharpened lever arms attached to both feet; two to four hours riding in a car or bus; and, finally, sitting on a chair lift for 5 to 15 minutes with five or more pounds suspended from each leg. Under these circumstances, the fact that only 1 percent of the skiers will be injured on any given day is providential.

The frequency of ski injuries is usually reported as the number of injuries per 1000 ski man-days (SMD); thus an injury rate of 3.8 per 1000 SMD would mean that slightly less than 0.4 percent of the skiers were injured. Injury rates in the United States hover around 10 per 1000 SMD. If one just counts those injured skiers seeking aid from the ski patrol or first-aid facility at a ski area, the injury rate is between 3 and 4 per 1000 SMD. For whatever reason, not all injured skiers seek aid at the time of injury. Indeed, some do not even realize that they have been injured. Recent studies indicate that less than half of those individuals injured severely enough to disrupt their normal activities are examined at ski patrol or first-aid facilities.

Note that not only do minor injuries go untended at the ski resort but also as many as a quarter of the fractures and up to one-third of the knee injuries requiring surgical treatment bypass medical or first-aid facilities at the ski area. The most inclusive studies would place the overall injury rate* at around 10 per 1000 SMD or 1 percent (of the skiers on a given day) with between 25 to 40 percent of the injured receiving medical or first-aid care at the ski area.

Many investigations have been undertaken in attempts to identify the factors that are related to an increased likelihood of injury. Everything about skiers has been studied, from their drinking habits to their frustrations in traffic enroute to the ski area. As one might imagine in dealing with a sport where injuries are treated in such a cavalier manner, myths and "old wives tales" are legion. Because all

---

*Injury defined as a traumatic, medical condition arising from skiing and resulting in disruption of normal activities.

skiers have either been injured or acquainted with someone who has been injured, the tendency to generalize from personal experiences is great. "Brand X bindings are the safest because my wife and I've skied in them for twenty years and we've never been hurt" is a commonly heard "scientific conclusion" among skiers.

Before discussing what factors are related to a greater likelihood of injury, it is appropriate to differentiate between skiing *accidents* and skiing *injuries.* Accidents are unforeseen occurrences and have been experienced by every skier. Most falls are accidental. Notably, most falls do not produce injuries. An injury, then, is an accident "gone bad." The occurrence of an injury usually implies a preceding accident; the converse is usually not true. It might be legitimately said that accident-free skiing is injury-free. One can go one step further and state that failing to fall generally means injury-free skiing, since more than 85 percent of ski injuries are the result of falling.

The distinction between accidents (usually falling) and injuries is important because the variables discussed here might be related to the occurrence of accidents and not injuries or vice versa. In some cases, some characteristic might influence both the occurrence of accidents and injuries; in others, the relationships are obscure. The following are generalities related to ski safety. Some may be modified by the skiers themselves, others can only be warily observed.

Better skiers are less likely to be injured. True. Generally, the more expert a skier becomes, the less likely he or she is to be injured. Female skiers progressively decrease their injury rates with each increment in expertise. Thus female intermediates ski more safely than beginners and experts more safely than intermediates. In males, the linearity of the expertise-safety relationship is not as marked. Both intermediates and experts appear to ski more safely than beginners but the progression from intermediate to expert is unaccompanied by any appreciable decrease in injury rates.

The more experienced skier is a safer skier. True. Regardless of whether or not more years of skiing are accompanied by more expertise, just the fact that the skier has endured two or more years appears to result in a decreased likelihood of being injured. If more experience is accompanied by greater expertise, all the better.

Adults ski more safely than children. Generally true. This may be partly because older people (adults) have had more opportunity to become experienced or expert skiers. Even when this is taken into account, youth – especially "teen-age" youth – seems to be associated with higher injury rates.

In the past few years, it has been suggested that children may account for an increased share of skiing injuries. This is particularly difficult to document because children's injuries are much more likely to be reported to (and treated by) ski patrols. Thus higher children's injury rates may be, at least in part, artifactual.

Because of their skeletal immaturity, children sustain different injuries than adults; and, in part, this might explain the apparently higher injury rates.

For example, forces resulting in a ligament injury (sprain) in the adult knee might result in an epiphyseal (growth center) fracture in the child, with the latter being more spectacular and, therefore, more likely to be seen in the ski areas, ski patrol, or first-aid facility.

Females have a higher injury rate than males. Probably true for recreational skiers. It would appear that when one corrects for influences of expertise, experience, and age, females are slightly more likely to be injured than males. The only exception is the competitive female skier who enjoys an injury rate similar to her male counterpart.

No one has adequately explained why females have higher injury rates. It has been suggested that their "bones are lighter" and thus "fracture more easily" but the bones are not disproportionately "light" in relationship to total body weight. Even if these observations were valid, an increase in fractures alone would not increase the injury rates enough to explain the male/female differences.

Taking ski lessons decreases the likelihood of being injured. Probably, but in a less than direct way. It is possible to document the fact that formal instruction accelerates the acquisition of expertise, and this expertise is accompanied by a decreased injury rate. This decrease occurs over time and is not an immediate effect of the lessons.

Time spent skiing during lessons may well be safer than free skiing, but this is because – especially during beginner and intermediate phases – one does not ski much during lessons.

Skiing on wet snow (or deep powder or ice or packed snow) causes more ski injuries. Nobody knows. From a mechanical standpoint, wet, heavy snow seems more likely to "trap" or fail to release an errant ski and thus increase the likelihood of injury. The association of ski injuries with particular snow conditions is difficult to document since, at almost any time, many varying snow conditions simultaneously exist at any particular ski area. There may indeed be some association between these conditions and frequency of injuries but documentation of it is almost impossible.

The "last run" of the day is the most dangerous. Somewhat facetiously, the run during which you are injured is usually the "last run" of that particular day. This statement implies that skiing late in the day is more dangerous (than earlier in the day). It is true that time periods during middle and late afternoon account for more ski injuries than similar time periods in the morning. This is not because the afternoon is more dangerous for the individual skier, but because there are more people skiing (at risk) in the afternoon than in the morning.

Skiing when fatigued results in an increased likelihood of injury. Intuitively, there seems to be little argument with this statement, however, "fatigue" in the skier is difficult to assess. Many skiers are so poorly conditioned that all of their skiing occurs while "fatigued." The well-conditioned pleasure skiers, on the other hand, may only rarely exert themselves to the point of fatigue. Studies over the past few years have revealed that a "day of skiing" can involve from 20 minutes to six hours of activity and, usually, the true "ski day" should be measured in minutes rather than hours.

Skiing in "flat light" is more dangerous. Difficult to assess. "Flat light" is really any condition (clouds, fog, sheltered areas, etc.) that results in an absence of shadows or tangential light, which makes terrain features difficult to discern. Surely, skiing on a surface that one cannot see is less than ideal from a safety standpoint but, at the same time, it is difficult to avoid these situations completely. Most skiers approach the sport with more caution when they cannot see and this seems to be an appropriate approach. There seems to be no justification for such measures as area closure because of lighting conditions.

RECOGNITION OF SKIING INJURIES

The injured skier is probably more fortunate than any other recreational athlete. Only intercollegiate athletes who are cared for by their Athletic Trainers receive diagnostic care and first aid comparable to that given to skiers by professional ski patrolmen or members of the National Ski Patrol System; but even the highly skilled and specific ministrations delivered by the ski patrol are of no avail if injured skiers do not present themselves for care.

In spite of their remarkable capabilities and ready availability, the services of the ski patrol are utilized by approximately a third of the injured skiers. The ski patrol is occasionally avoided because of embarrassment on the part of the injured. Usually, however, skiers simply do not realize that they have been significantly injured on leaving the ski area. The snow and cold serve as effective deterrents against pain and swelling, often masking the injury. An hour or so in a warm car or a sauna or heated pool results in painful swelling and stiffness at a time when no medical assistance is readily available. If one suspects an injury, the best time for a professional evaluation of its severity is as near the time of the injury as possible.

The most troublesome of the seemingly mild injuries is that resulting in a tear of the medial collateral (inside) ligament of the knee. The most severe of these particular injuries are often painless after the first few seconds. Skiers, realizing they have been injured, are relieved to find that they can bear weight on their knee without pain. Attempts to ski or walk are often met with a painless sense of instability or "wobble" in the knee. The feeling of instability in a weight-bearing joint (hip, knee, or ankle) is almost always indicative of a major injury, regardless of whether or not it is accompanied by pain, and it should be medically evaluated immediately. If the injury requires surgical repair, the operation should be carried out in the first few days after the injury. More than one skier has come out of this situation with a permanently unstable knee because he or she thought an initially painless injury could not be severe in spite of increased pain, swelling, and stiffness over the ensuing week.

Other injuries often ignored are those of the hand and wrist. Fractures of the small bones of the hand and wrist are not uncommon in skiers and some, if ignored, can result in degenerative arthritis and permanent disability.

A good rule of thumb for skiing —or any recreational sport-injury is that if the arm or leg does not function or look like its opposite side, the skier should find out why. Thus, such conditions as obvious swelling, loss of motion, pain with motion, loss of strength or numbness or tingling usually indicate that something is wrong. These conditions should be evaluated by some one knowledgeable in dealing with these problems. Another good rule is that when one hears a "snap" or "pop" or has the sensation of "something tearing" or "ripping," generally some major supporting structure (tendon or ligament) has been injured. The same rules are true for the skier who returns to the slopes following an injury. If it is impossible to ski comfortably, then it is probably equally impossible to ski safely and more rehabilitation is necessary.

SECTION 4
Analysis of Skier Needs

Skiing has been described (6) as a sport in which sharp-edged lever arms are attached to the feet for the purpose of sliding down an inclined plane that has a surface of varying density, from powder snow to rock, and frequently contains foreign bodies such as lift towers and trees. This tongue-in-cheek description provides a nearly perfect general analysis of the sport and could be improved upon only by emphasizing the existing variability in the inclined planes or slopes. In keeping with Phase I of optimum training procedures, that is, characterizing the sport, as outlined in Section 5, a more detailed analysis is needed here.

A comprehensive analysis of the sport will someday include a biomechanical analysis of each skill. Although such an analysis is beyond the scope of this book, we will outline many of the muscular, physiological, and neuropsychological "ingredients" that make up the sport. Skiers who attend to these needs and work to correct weaknesses will be best able to endure and master the mechanical skills of skiing. We recognize that the specific needs are proportionally different for skiers of differing levels of ability but feel that the following are essential in some degree for all skiers from novices through competitive racers.

MUSCULAR CONSIDERATIONS

Basic needs in this area are for at least a minimum level of muscular strength and endurance in localized regions of the body. To meet these basic levels allows skiers to begin skiing with the knowledge that they will be capable of performing basic skills without excessive muscular fatigue or muscle soreness. This can serve as a great confidence builder. It can also minimize the risk of injury to joints through the protection that strong, nonfatigued, and enduring muscles provide. Most young people can pass tests for minimum muscular strength and endurance as can older persons who have remained physically active. Unfortunately, these categories do not include many people of all ages who decide to take up skiing. Figures 2, 3, and 4 show the major muscle groups used in skiing and indicate the type of training that would specifically meet the functional demands placed on each group (optimal training).

A review of the training-needed columns of Figures 2 to 4 indicates that skiing involves a static contraction of many muscle groups, that is, an isometric holding by many muscle groups instead of dynamic contractions resulting in limb movements, as needed in other sports. Furthermore, the static holding must be endured for prolonged periods, with only slight modifications in muscle length or joint position, which emphasizes the need for static endurance training. A close review of the many functions of the front thigh muscles (quadriceps) indicates that these powerful muscles are the foundation for good ski technique. The quadriceps provide the power for raising and lowering the body with speed, precision, and control and therefore must possess qualities of dynamic strength. Since these dynamic contractions are repeated in rapid succession, it is also important that the quadriceps are trained to improve their dynamic endurance capabilities. Finally, since the thigh muscles support the body in a partially flexed position during straight running, they must be able to endure this static holding, which emphasizes the need for static endurance training. The importance of the second group of muscles, the hip angulators, for edging, heel thrust, and leg angulation has been discussed by Wilson (7). Optimum training exercises have been included for these abductor, adductor, and rotator muscles, which lie deep in the hip-groin region of the body. The abductors pull the thigh away from the body midline while the adductors pull the thigh inward. Contraction of the rotators causes inward or outward rotation of the thigh around its long axis.

It should be clear that Figures 2 to 4 do not contain all of the muscles involved in skiing, but only the major groups. There are many additional muscles that contribute to movements as secondary movers or that stabilize or neutralize during the contraction of primary movers. In Section 7, specific training procedures will be defined to condition the muscles of the major groups. Since many of these calisthenics and exercises are purposely designed to mimic the movements and static holds performed during skiing, we feel that the secondary muscle groups involved will also receive optimum training.

Most of the preceding material of this section has been a discussion of the muscular needs for skiing and identification of optimum training to best meet those needs. Skiers should readily recognize that frequent strains, pains, and limitations to performance are not because of a response failure of the muscles but can be related to connective tissue. Three types of connective tissues of most interest here are tendons, ligaments, and cartilage. In brief, tendons allow muscular pulling forces to be transmitted to bones through their direct connection, ligaments add stability to joints through their attachment to the bones on either side, and cartilage buffers the impact of jolts and allows for smooth and directed sliding movements of bones at joints. Since excessive forces can result in strains, partial tears, and even ruptures of these connective tissues, it is important that skiers attend to their special needs.

Since most muscle-conditioning exercises emphasize the contraction instead of the relaxation aspect of training, there is a tendency for muscles to shorten as they become stronger. This partially accounts for the extremes in body build and posture seen in some weight lifters, wrestlers, and other athletes who have diligently trained and competed over a period of several years. If this shortening results in a reduction in the range of motion or increases the potential for muscle or tendon strains or tears, then the trainee should practice muscle-stretching exercises as well as strength- and endurance-conditioning exercises.

A second good reason for performing stretching exercises on a regular basis has mainly to do with ligaments. These tough sections of connective tissue do not stretch much when subjected to rapidly applied forces and therefore constrain or set the limits of movement

	BODY AREA	MAJOR MUSCLES	ACTION	PURPOSE	TRAINING NEEDED
1	Abdomen	Rectus Abdominis	Trunk flexion	Holding ski posture	Static endurance
2	Groin	Many adductors	Thighs together	Hold leg position	Static endurance
3	Buttocks	Gluteals	Hip extension	Pelvic thrust	Dynamic and Static strength endurance
4	Upper leg (back)	Hamstrings	Assist hip extension	Pelvic thrust	Static endurance
5	Lower leg (outer)	Peroneus Longus	Inward ankle roll	Assist in edging	Static endurance

FIGURE 2. Major muscle groups used in wedge position with an indication of type of training viewed as optimal.

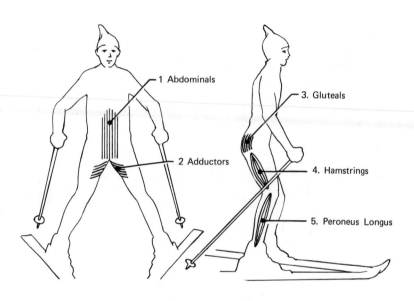

1 Abdominals

2 Adductors

3. Gluteals

4. Hamstrings

5. Peroneus Longus

27

	BODY AREA	MAJOR MUSCLES	ACTION	PURPOSE	TRAINING NEEDED
6	Neck	Spinalis	Neck extension	Maintain head position	Static endurance
7	Shoulder and chest	Deltoids and Pectorals	Upper arm extension	Vigorous poling	Dynamic strength
8	Upper arms (back part)	Triceps	Lower arm extension	Poling, getting up	Dynamic strength and endurance
9	Lower arm and hand	Many flexors	Wrist flexion and grip	Grip pole, rope tow	Static strength and endurance
10	Lateral back	Latissimus	Upper arm extension	Vigorous poling	Dynamic endurance
11	Lower back	Many deep extensors	Trunk extension	Holding ski position	Static endurance
12	Upper leg (front part)	Quadriceps	Lower leg extension	Hold, raise and lower body	Static and dynamic strength and endurance
13	Lower leg (back part)	Gastrocnemius (calf)	Foot extension	Position leg in boot	Static endurance and stretching

FIGURE 3. Additional major muscle groups used in basic, straight running position with an indication of type of training viewed as optimal.

28

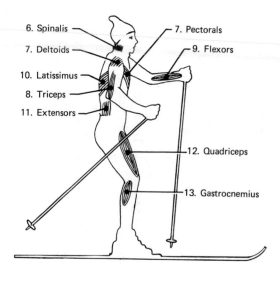

6. Spinalis

7. Deltoids

10. Latissimus

8. Triceps

11. Extensors

7. Pectorals

9. Flexors

12. Quadriceps

13. Gastrocnemius

	BODY AREA	MAJOR MUSCLES	ACTION	PURPOSE	TRAINING NEEDED
14	Lower back	Quadratus Lumborum	Trunk lateral flexion	Angulation to maintain balanced C of G	Dynamic strength and static endurance
15	Medial back	Sacrospinalis	Trunk rotation	Initiate turning power, maintain C of G	Dynamic strength and static endurance
16	Abdomen	Obliques and Rectus Abdominus	Trunk flexion and rotation	Initiate and block turning power	Static strength
17	Groin	Abductors and adductors	Thigh angulation	Edging	Dynamic strength and static endurance
18	Hip	Internal and external rotators	Thigh rotation	Heel thrust	Dynamic strength
19	Leg	Flexors and extensors	Flexion and extension at knee	Unweighting	Dynamic strength and endurance
20	Lower leg	Tibialis Anterior and Posterior	Outward ankle roll	Assist in edging	Static endurance

FIGURE 4. Additional requirements, as are used in down--- skiing techniques with an indication of types of training

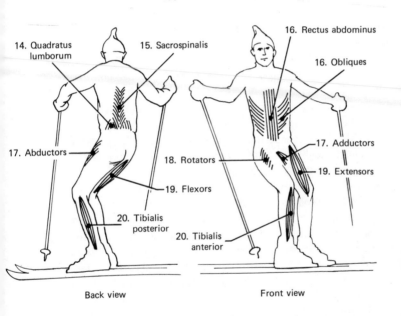

14. Quadratus lumborum

15. Sacrospinalis

16. Rectus abdominus

16. Obliques

17. Abductors

17. Adductors

18. Rotators

19. Flexors

19. Extensors

20. Tibialis posterior

20. Tibialis anterior

Back view

Front view

for many joints. This is especially true for the spine, where the ligamentous structure is widespread and has many overlapping ligaments along the vertebral bodies. These ligaments tend to shorten and become stiffer with aging. Adhesions can also develop between ligaments or between their fibers, particularly during healing from minor tears, and thereby contribute to a stiffened, nonflexible spine. Since the performance of stretching exercises on a regular basis can greatly reduce the development of adhesions and possibly forestall natural aging effects, it makes good sense to do them. The desirable outcome of doing such stretching exercises would be a protection of the flexibility, extensibility, and rotational capabilities of the trainee's spine. This is of particular importance in our American culture, where few citizens must work hard physically in order to earn a living. With this approach, it has seemingly become expected and accepted that spines will stiffen at an early age and that we should all expect to experience episodes of low back pain. It is unfortunate since, in truth, many of these limitations to spinal function may be self-imposed, that is, the time period during which we develop spinal rigidity is when we have also decided to no longer make an effort to retain our youthful flexibility.

Stretching exercises can be done in a variety of ways. A movement technique (sometimes called dynamic or ballistic stretching) involves stretching to within a few inches of the limits of movement for the joint or joints and then moving repeatedly through this range of constraint. Some have referred to the final movements of this technique as bounce stretching or "bouncing" and feel that there is an inherent danger of overstraining associated connective tissue. Others have suggested that a known protective-inhibition reflex is activated with such stretching, so that desirable stretching effects are neutralized by contraction and shortening of the muscles undergoing stretch. These arguments have led many therapists to discontinue using dynamic stretching exercises in favor of static stretching. We feel that dynamic stretching still has an important place in flexibility conditioning, maintenance, and rehabilitation training, since it emphasizes the application of on-off forces rather than the application of a steady deforming force. If extensibility changes or adaptations prove to be specific to the type of stretching practiced during training, then some dynamic stretching would be indicated in preparation for sports. This is especially true for sports like skiing, which involve strenuous, localized muscular contractions, much body and limb motion, and additional hazards to tendons and ligaments as a result of deforming dynamic forces experienced during falls or because of equipment leverage, for example, the forces "felt" at joints are usually sudden and excessive during a fall or when a skier "catches" an edge.

Static stretching involves movement to the constraining limits of a joint, that is, until resistance is felt in some area of the system, and then stretching just beyond this point and holding steadily for a given count (usually 10 to 15 seconds). Participants must be cautioned against overstraining just as they must be warned against "bouncing" too vigorously during dynamic stretching. The goal of either approach is to be able to stretch a bit further after each week or month of practice. These time units put the expected outcomes in proper perspective, since participants should not expect miraculous overnight results but should rather be content with gains that can reasonably be measured in fractions of inches over a few weeks.

Stretching and flexibility exercises should be performed each day, if possible, and at least three times a week. They can usually best be done after rising in the morning or as part of a conditioning workout. If they are included as part of a workout, they can be used to good advantage to loosen up and relax muscles or as part of a cooling-down routine. They can also be interspersed between strenuous weight lifting or calisthenic exercises so that the trainee is doing something while recovering from localized fatigue. A final application is to use stretching exercises to loosen up muscles and joints after injury or during the process of rehabilitation. If the injury has been at all severe, this is frequently the only type of activity that can be tolerated. Once again, the goal is to stretch and increase range of motion without producing additional trauma or inflammation. Kraus (8) has emphasized the need for this type of flexibility retraining during recovery from ski injuries.

Section 7 contains descriptions of several stretching exercises that are recommended because they provide for stretching and loosening of all major muscle and joint areas of the body. These areas include (1) the neck, shoulders, and chest, (2) the upper spine and low back region, (3) the abdominal and lateral trunk region, (4) the buttocks, quadriceps, and thigh adductors, and (5) the calf, Achilles tendon and front of lower leg regions. If these stretching exercises are interspersed throughout the preseason and year-round workouts of skiers, there is little doubt that significant gains in joint flexibility will be realized. For best effect, they should be performed on a very regular basis and, if possible, become part of a person's daily exercise program. If this is done, the performer will likely acquire benefits to agility, flexibility, and spinal health that are felt and enjoyed year-round, as well as during the ski season.

PHYSIOLOGICAL CONSIDERATIONS

The physiological needs and responses of skiers are highly variable, depending on the skiers' skill level, the intensity with which the sport is being pursued, the terrain that is skied, and their physical fitness level. Since the same slopes can be skied by advanced skiers for the most rapid rate of descent or by the less skilled for control and turning practice with frequent rest stops, it is difficult to describe the sport as one that requires high or low levels of energy expenditure. Although this characteristic of the sport makes categorization difficult, it contributes greatly to the numbers who can enjoy skiing, that is, people of all ages and levels of skill can enjoy an activity that has the same common basis. Within this framework, the energy cost of participating can be viewed as a sliding scale that decreases as technical skills improve and increases as skiers are able to demand their bodies to perform runs that are not only longer and faster but require more energy output to perform advanced techniques. A system of progression and regression of energy-expenditure levels is also inherent in the variety of slopes that are available, since a person could reasonably progress to skiing advanced slopes and then voluntarily regress to advanced intermediate or intermediate slopes in later years.

Most athletic activities are now categorized into those that are predominantly aerobic or anaerobic. The term aerobic means that the rate of oxygen uptake is adequate to meet the oxygen needs of the working body cells as they utilize energy substrates of carbohydrates and fats. During aerobic work, athletes are functioning in a physiological steady state and can endure the activity for prolonged periods of time, for example, a cross-country ski race or marathon run. Consequently, in common usage, the term aerobic has become synonomous with low intensity—long duration work. By contrast, the term anaerobic describes energy production and work performance where the quantities of oxygen made available to or utilized by working cells is less than adequate, and the performer cannot function within the framework of a physiological steady state and is forced to draw on limited quantities of stored energy. For this reason, all-out predominantly anaerobic performances cannot be endured for more than 10 to 30 seconds without loss of speed, for example, an uphill ski sprint or a 400-yard running sprint. In common usage, then, the term anaerobic is used to describe athletic performances of high intensity but short duration.

It is important to recognize that most activities do or can have both aerobic and anaerobic aspects or components, and when they are described as being either one or the other, it is really just a general description of the predominant form of energy metabolism that is being made. For example, a skier may elect to leisurely traverse the first one-third of a mile-long run and "race" the final two-thirds. In this case, the first part of the run would be predominantly a submaximal-aerobic effort whereas the final run would be more anaerobic. In fact, depending on the terrain and the technical skill of the performer, an all-out race at the end may stress the energy production systems (both aerobic and anaerobic) to their limits and leave the skier in a state of temporary fatigue.

As indicated above, it is difficult to categorize skiing as being predominantly an aerobic or anaerobic activity, and there is no good reason for attempting to do so. The young beginner who is schussing the bunny slope is functioning aerobically as is the elderly skilled skier who descends the intermediate slope using broad, lazy traverses. By contrast, the intermediate or advanced skiers who are aggressively charging slopes barely within the limits of their skill are functioning more anaerobically. As their skill increases, they can descend the same slope just as rapidly or slightly faster using less anaerobic and more aerobic metabolism. If they choose to ski the same slope at a faster rate, they will again resort to a more anaerobic metabolism.

Skiing is an anaerobic activity for many skiers. This statement includes those who aggressively ski rather short, well-groomed, and frequently man-made slopes in the midwest where top-to-bottom time may be as short as 20 seconds. It also includes skiers who ski mountain powder as vigorously as possible and must stop for frequent rests. In either case, the forced or voluntary high-intensity work is of comparatively short duration. From a physiological standpoint, it is important to ask: "Why does a skier stop to rest?" "Why do some skiers need to rest so frequently while others seemingly go on forever?" Most skiers stop to rest when they perceive a level of localized muscle fatigue or joint strain where they feel it would not be enjoyable and, it might be hazardous for them to continue skiing at the same intensity. Others sense their rapid, labored breathing and perceive it as an indication that they may be overexerting themselves and should take a breather. Frequently, these perceptions of exertion occur when anxiety over falling is beginning to peak, when vision is becoming blurred, and more mistakes in technique are being made. If skiers are unnecessarily rigid and tense, this will contribute greatly to their energy-expenditure rate and result in a faster onset of fatigue. Consider the middle-aged woman who becomes nearly exhausted while sliding and poling from the ski rental shop to the rope tow for the first time.

In summary, when most skiers stop to rest, it is because of localized muscular fatigue that results from work done at a rate or intensity that exceeds the individual's capabilities to provide energy by aerobic means. They have had to start working anaerobically, and the duration of this work is limited by the quantities of energy reserves in the muscles. When these reserves are used at a rate faster than they can be replenished, the outcome is fatigue. If skiers did not stop to rest and replenish their energy reserves, they would soon become extremely fatigued and exhausted with loss of coordinated function leading to falls, collisions, and possible injuries. Skiers usually stop before such high levels of fatigue are encountered and, although they may be momentarily breathless, they are not experiencing the same degree of general exhaustion experienced by the competitive, long-distance runners or cross-country skiers at the end of a race. Recovery is quite rapid and, after a short pause or a ride up the lift, they are ready to go at an all-out pace again.

Now, let us consider the question of why some skiers can complete long runs down difficult slopes with only infrequent rest stops. The answer resides in individual differences in skill as well as in the level of conditioning or fitness of the skier. Since a well-conditioned body is the foundation that allows skill to be developed at a maximum rate, it becomes the single most important consideration in explaining the differences in endurance. Agnevik and Saltin (9) have studied the physical work capacity of young male and female competitive skiers who compete in the giant slalom and downhill races. Since these racers must be capable of skiing at top speed for two to three minutes, we can gain some perspective from measures of their fitness level, work capacities, and physiological responses during skiing. They were first tested in a research laboratory where they pedalled a bicycle against a preset resistance to yield measures of their maximum heart rates and maximum areobic power. An individual's maximum aerobic power ($\dot{V}O_2$ maximum) is determined by measuring the maximum amount of oxygen that they can utilize in a one-minute period while working at full intensity. The minute volume is then expressed in either absolute terms such as liters per minute (e.g., $\dot{V}O_2$ maximum = 4.2 liters per minute) or relative to body weight in kilograms (e.g., $\dot{V}O_2$ maximum = 60 milliliters per kilogram X minute). Measurements of maximum ventilation-volume rate, blood lactate, and leg and knee strength were also made. Maximum ventilation-volume rate is a measure of the amount of air moved into and out of the skier's lungs per minute, whereas blood lactic-acid measures provide an indirect estimate of anaerobic metabolism. After baseline values for these measures were established in the laboratory tests, additional evaluations were made during or immediately after skiers completed downhill racing events. Heart rate telemetry apparatus was used during the races to measure heart rates, and these rates were related to known heart rate versus oxygen consumption plots to estimate energy expenditure rates during skiing. These data indicate that maximum laboratory heart rates ranging from 198 to 207 beats per minute were met or exceeded after 20 to 50 seconds of special slalom, giant slalom, or downhill racing. Estimates of oxygen-consumption rate indicated aerobic metabolism at approximately 85 percent of maximum, a value that probably would have equaled the true maximum if events had lasted longer than 45 to 130 seconds. Strength measures indicated that the skiers possessed extremely strong quadriceps muscles. In fact, their maximum isometric strength performances for the leg press and knee extension exceeded those of weight lifters who were also tested.

Data from Agnevik and Saltin's studies reinforce the need for training for the anaerobic aspects of downhill skiing, since both the heart rate and blood-lactate responses indicated that high-intensity work was being performed. Although similar data are not available for intermediate and expert recreational skiers, it is likely that near maximum anaerobic performances would be common in both groups. It seems reasonable that expert recreational skiers would utilize their energy more efficiently in rapid descent of slopes but would more than make up for the difference because of less favorable snow, more obstacles, and more rugged terrain.

The data also emphasize the importance of aerobic training for serious skiers. Once again, aerobic function is the metabolic foundation on which any endurance activity is based. The skier possessing good aerobic power benefits in at least three ways. First, most endurance athletes have gained their endurance through workouts involving their legs. Therefore, their legs are in good shape and can likely exert strong, powerful contractions as well as endure activity for long periods of time. Second, the skier with greater aerobic power can function aerobically a greater portion of the time during any ski activities ranging from low to high intensity, that is, they do not depend so much on the provision of energy through anaerobic metabolism. And, third, skiers who are in better aerobic condition (cardiorespiratory fitness) recover much more quickly from high-intensity tasks that required them to utilize anaerobic reserves.

Considering the above, it is not difficult to understand why a truly well-conditioned skier can endure seemingly long, fast runs through powder snow and obstacles and appear well recovered at the finish. In skiing, as in most other sports, it makes sense to build your final special training on a physiological foundation that already includes a generally high level of overall physical fitness. It is for these reasons that a year-round cardiorespiratory training program followed by specific preseason conditioning exercises will be recommended in Sections 6 and 7. The ultimate in training approaches is to maintain the muscular and cardiorespiratory systems in a good status of functional tone and flexibility and then add the special conditioning and warm-up activities specific to each sport as you change seasons or go from sport to sport. As a result, it is obvious that you will end up with athletes who are never really out of condition and are surprised at how easily they move into and tolerate changes in sports. Oh what bliss!

NEUROPSYCHOLOGICAL CONSIDERATIONS

When an analysis of the important ingredients of a sport is made, the neuropsychological factors are frequently passed over entirely. Part of the reason for the omission is that many analysts view neural function as an inate matter that is present in varying degrees and that cannot be easily altered through training. An individual either has good coordination or does not, and there is little that can be done to improve the existing level of basic coordination. Furthermore, the reflexes essential to balance and coordination are not easily observable and are difficult, if not impossible, to measure. Finally, the impact of minute improvements in reflexes and reactions are frequently masked by what is seen as an improvement in gross motor skill, which is unquestionably the result of a combination of muscular, physiological, and neuropsychological improvements.

Our intention is to define a number of neuropsychological qualities important to skiers in an effort to make the reader more sensitive to these needs. In most cases, the matter of how best to improve on these qualities has not been defined, and it is assumed that much improvement occurs as a result of trial-and-error practice on the ski slopes.

Balance. It is a quality mediated by the sensory receptors of the inner ear (labyrinthine organ), which indicates that an individual's head is rapidly changing position, that is, losing one's balance. There is perception of direction of loss as well as rate of change of loss, and appropriate muscles are reflexly stimulated to contract to regain balance. It is fortunate that muscle contractions are reflexly inititated, since there would not be adequate time to think deeply about the appropriate action to take to prevent a fall.

Coordination. Smooth, coordinated, and appropriate muscle contractions, holds, and relaxations are a result of the coordinated integration of voluntary neural impulses and feedback reflexes from a variety of sensory receptors in the body. These receptors are located throughout muscles (muscle spindles), in the region of joints (joint receptors), in tendons (golgi organ), and in the pads of the feet (pressure receptors). These systems are important, since it is not enough for skiers to simply initiate muscle contractions to produce movements of a static holding of portions of their bodies; they also need nearly instantaneous feedback on whether the desired movement or tension has been attained. Furthermore, the term coordination implies that simultaneous muscular contractions will take place in proper sequence and with proper force in various regions of the body. Much of this coordinated function occurs within the cerebellum of the brain.

Agility. It can be defined as an individual's ability to control their body mass while moving and changing directions so that the transitions are smooth and efficient. There is considerable independence between this characteristic and those of balance and coordination, that is, a skier may have quite good balance and coordination but lack good agility. People with poor agility frequently display "sluggish legs" or "heavy feet" and expend considerable energy in maintaining or regaining their balance when attempting to alter the direction of their movement or change movement planes. Sometimes poor agility can be related to factors other than neuromuscular function, such as general lack of flexibility or muscular strength, and the ratio of strength to body mass. For example, it is difficult to display good agility if one's spine has become stiff and inflexible or if one has excessive body fat to both carry and control during movement. It is important to note that agility is greatly impaired as muscles begin to fatigue and cramp or during recovery from strains and sprains.

Timing. To ski expertly requires a good sense of timing, that is, a learned (usually through trial and error) ability to initiate and execute a movement at a time most favorable to producing a desired outcome. This is apparent in timing the moment of unweighting or lift off to the mogul, in optimum pole planting, in beginning turns as well as in boarding and leaving a fast moving chair lift. Since there is a sound, biomechanical basis for most maneuvers that have a critical timing aspect, the rudiments could easily be explained in "classroom" sessions before real practice is attempted. This should reasonable reduce the number of trial-and-error practices, frequently having a high injury-risk index, needed to gain an appreciation for the importance of situational timing in skiing.

Judgment. In high velocity sports like skiing where little protective gear is worn, matters of judgement related to self-preservation of life and limb take on a high level of importance. The base of reference for making appropriate judgements is usually information that can be recalled from previous experiences either in an identical situation or in one having significant carry-over similarity. In unusual or potentially dangerous situations, a skier will elect a course of action and usually follow through with it. For example, they may encounter unexpected heavy powder or ice, a narrow passage, other skiers or obstacles, or have to decide on a choice of descent routes. In making a decision, they will rely heavily on their memory of the outcome of previous, similar experiences; they may also reflect quickly on alternative courses of action and, hopefully, will always relate their choice to their own self-limitations and capabilities. Classroom "exposure" can also be helpful here, but it is seldom adequately provided, for example, less skilled skiers might more readily elect less difficult descent routes if made aware that it is the wisest course of action and has more to do with skiing skill and safety than any index of cowardice. Such knowledge should reduce the numbers of "peer pressure" groups who ski the same slopes without regard for differences in individual abilities. It also makes sense to expose students to higher risk situations while under close supervision by instructors so that they can be effectively criticized for errors in judgement.

Readiness. This neuropsychological quality also has a physiological aspect. In essence, when skiers declare either silently or verbally that they are ready, from both a psychological and physiological standpoint they "feel" ready and confident about what they are going to attempt. An appreciation for the existance of this characteristic and for the fact that it varies considerably among individuals is important and has implications during both instruction and practice. In terms of injury potential, it is sheer folly to "push" any skier into attempting a maneuver until they are ready. It makes sense then to tell students that they may "pass" and go to the rear of the line if they don't feel ready when their turn comes. This should allow them to build confidence within themselves by watching others, by hearing critical remarks from the instructor, and by thinking through the movement techniques. Skiers also vary greatly in the amount and type of warm-up they need before they feel ready. This undoubtedly has to do with physiological responsiveness and feelings of looseness that accompany warm-up activities. Finally, in terms of fatigue, no one knows better than the skiers themselves how ready they may or may not be. These internal perceptions of localized or general fatigue are early warning signals of impending impairments in performance, and they must be heeded by the participants since they usually occur somewhat before any outward signs—loss of coordination or timing—become apparent.

Desire. A quality that varies greatly both within and across individuals. It can be defined as a psychological drive to master a technique, to improve overall skill level, or simply as an individual's self-motivation to remain upright and keep their feet and skis as their base of support. Quantitative differences in this quality are expressed in the behavior of some particularly competitive people who practice frequently and diligently in an effort to be "the best," as opposed to others who aspire to a modest skill level, attain the desired level, and are content to remain and enjoy such participation. Since enjoyment of skiing, like most sports, is closely related to achievement of skill, most skiers initially possess a reasonable level of desire to acquire at least minimal competency. Thereafter, they tend to become stratified into performance classes, mainly because of the importance that they attach to reaching a higher class strata, especially in view of the amount of instruction, practice, and exposure to risks that such advancement would require.

Courage. This quality can be simply defined as a lack of fear. Although such a definition may fit some situations, it seems unreasonable to apply it to situations where alternative courses of action are available and acceptable. In skiing, a better expression of this quality would be the internal feelings of confidence that tell the skier that it's time to, for example, attempt the next challenge, to try the expert slope that has seemed so forbidding, and to enter that first race. This places the term courage into an operational framework of intelligence—courage—that is, each situation is internally judged relative to the confidence level of the individual and an appropriate fear response is made. Such an operational definition seems best, since we are generally apprehensive and fearful of any new situation where the outcome is unknown. In fact, we should be appropriately afraid of attempting activities having a high potential for self-injury until we have advanced through proper training and experience, which minimizes the inherent risk.

Aggressiveness. A quality that can be viewed as the opposite of cautiousness. It is frequently associated with individuals skiing beyond the limits of their technical skills but enjoying success because of compensations of strength, superb balance, or "natural" athletic ability. These skiers have not mastered the hill but are instead being taken for a ride by the hill. Many of them will progress very quickly if they choose to learn proper techniques (they usually have already experienced speed), but many also develop improper techniques that must be "unlearned" later. Most insutructors feel that it is good to be somewhat aggressive rather than extremely timid.

Although it is not so easy to train to improve the neuropsychological characteristics important to skiing, as it is the muscular and physiological characteristics, participants and instructors might consider the following points. First, a warning note on the hazards of mixing alcohol, drugs, and skiing. Many of these intoxicants are dangerous to use, since they slow responses and disturb balance, coordination, and orientation yet give the user a false sense of well-being and excellence of performance. This reduction in true performance can be coupled with some synergistic (combined effect greater than either single effect) effects of exercise, cold, and a reduced sensation of fatigue that render drug and alcohol usage an extremely dangerous practice while skiing. The best guideline here is to refrain from the use of intoxicants for eight hours before the lifts open in the morning and until they close in the afternoon. This reduces the hazard of quitting skiing for the day, having two or three drinks, then changing your mind and returning to the slopes. The schedule also allows for some rest and recovery time after the previous night's party. This appears essential, since some morning ski accident victims have been judged to be extremely unstable as a result of a heavy hangover.

Balance and coordination can be trained and improved in home or gymnasium workout sessions as well as during practice on the slopes. Two available, commercial devices that can be used to improve the types of balance and coordination needed in skiing are the Bongo Board and Ski Way. These stationary devices permit simulation of motions experienced in skiing and allow performers to practice the muscle control and body shifts needed to control balance. Some improvement in balance is also possible through participation in closely related sports such as water skiing, surfing, skating, and skate-board riding. Significant but lesser improvements can be realized from participation in more general sports involving whole-body movement, balance, and coordination such as handball, racquetball, volleyball, and gymnastics.

Agility as needed in skiing can be improved with calisthenics, which have an agility component as part of the movement. These drills also promote improvements in strength and explosive power—important in initiating proper raising and lowering of the body (can be viewed as trunk agility). Two such agility activities are the box jumping and leg flexion and extension exercises shown in Section 7, p. 00. Much additional improvement in agility can come through muscle strength, gained through general conditioning exercises and by keeping body weight down. Finally, teach students how to fall gracefully and agilely, both on the slopes and during indoor practice sessions on mats. During these indoor falling drills, participants should be taught how to relax while falling and rolling. Collapse falls, slide falls, side rolls, and shoulder rolls should be taught from both a stationary position and after running a short distance. Using proper technique, even a fall can be viewed as a graceful, coordinated finale to an otherwise ordinary ski run. It's all a matter of how you view it.

The matters of timing, readiness, and judgement are, for the most part, learned through experience. This trial-and-error method can be greatly improved on since, as someone has said, "experience is a cruel teacher since the examination is given first and then the lession." Unfortunately, in the course of skiing, the examination can have such objective "grades" as broken bones, sprained joints, wrenched knees, and lacerations when performances in timing, readiness, or judgement are poor. Certainly, any qualified instructor has the needed background and experience to alert his or her pupils to some of the situations where attention must be given to timing and readiness. It will also help if some classroom time is spent discussing some of the hazards of overskiing beyond one's ability, in compliance with pressure from an instructor or from peers. In doing this, attention is not only given to the matter of judgement but also to the aspects of desire, courage, and aggressiveness as previously outlined. These discussions do much to relieve irrelevant pressures that cloud rational decisions and create a larger body of intelligent and safety-conscious ski consumers. This educational step is the first and probably the most important one promoted by any agency who is interested in having participants assume a greater share of the responsibility for their own safety and that of others, especially in sports that are difficult to control.

SECTION 5
Optimum Training and Conditioning

APPROACH IMPORTANT

What do we mean by an optimum training approach? By definition, an optimum approach to training would be one that yields the greatest amount of improvement in the shortest amount of time, without creating any hazards or injuries to the person practicing the training techniques. With this in mind, the optimum training approach should have four main phases. Athletics coaches have recognized the importance of these phases in their attempts to optimize training programs for both amateur and professional athletes. Recreational athletes would also benefit greatly by paying attention to them since, in the final analysis, "athletics are athletics" and any modifiers like recreational, amateur, or professional merely denote other considerations such as skill level, intensity of participation, and money earned. The main point is that even recreational skiers will advance most rapidly by adhering to the following procedures in devising their own optimum training program.

Phase I. Characterize the Sport. Determine the major components or ingredients of the sport. On which factors does high-level, skillfull performance depend? How much tolerance for individual variability exists for these factors? How much allowance is permitted for compensatory shifts across factors? Major ingredients of skiing are agility, coordination, static-muscular endurance, flexibility, dynamic-muscular strength and endurance, technique, and courage. These terms have been previously defined in Section 4 under Analysis of Skier Needs, and it would be advantageous to read or review the definitions before proceeding. This applies particularly to recreational skiers who may be exposed to the terms for the first time.

Phase II. Assess the Performers' Weaknesses and Strengths. Apply valid field or laboratory tests to determine which individual factors are inhibiting or contributing to the current level of performance. Once these are known, a strategy to alter techniques to capitalize on strengths, or to define a training program that optimizes correction of weaknesses can be planned and carried out. Section 8 p. 000 contains a description of some field tests that would be appropriate for skiers to use to test themselves. These are tests of local muscle strength and endurance, of heart rate recovery after work, and of running ability as a measure of cardiorespiratory (aerobic) fitness. Some of the tests are more interesting and stimulating when performed in groups, but there is no reason why an individual could not self-test on all of them. Some of the tests are scored on a pass-fail basis, while performance rankings are given for others. On completion of all items, recreational skiers should better appreciate how in or out of shape they really are.

Phase III. Devise Optimum Training Practices. The term specificity of training implies that the outcome of training is specifically related to training input (the amount and type of activity done during training sessions). With regard to each performer, the closer the outcome or result of training specifically corrects weaknesses or improves technique, the closer the training can be regarded as optimum. Anyone who is really interested in improving in a sport would be foolish to use approaches that do not maximize the desired outcomes, results, improvements, or adaptations. Sections 6 and 7 contain information on year-round, general physical conditioning and special conditioning programs that will prove valuable to skiers at all levels of skill who are interested in devising optimun programs.

Phase IV. Reevaluate Performance. The important, final step to good training is to frequently reevaluate the performance of each participant. These evaluations can be made through field trials to to establish whether improvement has occurred, through results of competitions, and observations of performance technique, for example. A natural sequel to this reevaluation is a modification of training programs in which a majority of practice time is spent on improving persistent weaknesses. In organized athletics, these evaluations are made under the watchful eye of the coach and they also show up in performance times, distances thrown or jumped, and games won and lost. Recreational skiers may get some feedback from instructors or friends but will have to rely heavily on their own perceptions of their strength, stamina, chronic weaknesses, improved performance, and confidence. In view of these shortcomings, improvements should be much faster when an optimum approach to training is followed rather than proceeding with no plan or a scattergun approach. We assume, of course, that all skiers are interested in improving their skill, which we believe is a universally valid assumption. Yes — even if some say they are not interested — everyone would like to ski better because there is the key to even greater enjoyment.

PRINCIPLES ALSO IMPORTANT

There are also a few training principles that have a good scientific basis that should be taken into account when defining any training program or specific group of conditioning exercises. These basic principles are outlined below. If they are remembered during the review of selected preseason ski conditioning exercises (Section 7 p. 000), it will clearer why certain exercises were selected and others were excluded.

1. *"Specificity"* of training for general fitness indicates that aerobic (submaximal intensity work performed for long periods, such as running one to two miles) training best promotes improvements in cardiorespiratory endurance. Conversely, isometric training of muscle groups does little to improve C-R fitness. This serves as the rationale for our recommendations in Section 6, p. 00, Best Methods To Achieve Good Year-Round Physical Condition.

2. *"Specificity"* implies that the acts performed in resistance training for a specific sport should, as much as possible, *mimic* the

acts performed in execution of some aspect of the sport. Nearly all the conditioning exercises in Section 7, p. 66 adhere to this principle.

3. *"Specificity"* also indicates that the outcome of training will be specific to the input, that is, if isometric endurance training is practiced, the improvements will be in isometric endurance and, if dynamic endurance training is practiced, the improvements will be in dynamic endurance (10, 11). For this reason, exercises to improve both static and dynamic strength and endurance are included in Section 7, p. 000.

4. *"Specificity"* of muscle training indicates that when the desired outcome is muscular endurance, a large number (N = 12 to 15) of repetitions and sets (N = 6) should be performed. Conversely, when strength is the desired outcome, a small number of repetitions (N = 6) and sets (N = 3) should be done. This is the same as saying that light weights lifted many times will build endurance while strength can best be improved using heavy weights that can be lifted only a few times (12). The reader will see that a variety of exercise are included in Section 7, p. 000, some that only involve lifting a portion of body weight and others that involve the use of weights in a progressive resistance (weight-training) manner.

5. *Overloading* muscles is essential to stimulating increases in strength or endurance, that is, trainees must work against resistance. To meet this principle, all of the recommended conditioning exercises provide some form of overload resistance.

6. *Continued use* of muscles results in better maintenance of strength and bulk (hypertrophy), whereas disuse results in loss of strength, endurance, and size (atrophy). The importance of this principle is repeatedly emphasized in Section 6 (Year-Round Conditioning), since it applies somewhat to the maintenance of the performance capacity of other systems (heart, lungs, and blood vessels) as well as to muscles.

7. Strength and endurance training can frequently result in improvements in *functional capacity* without proportional changes in outward appearance, that is, muscle girths. The major points are that, although most people like to develop large muscles for appearance sake (not all desire to, especially some women) and

although there can be an injury protection advantage to having increased muscle mass and tone, it is really the improvement in muscle function that counts. In essence, we don't really care how much improvement there is in appearance—we are more interested in what the underlying muscles can do for us when called on to perform.

8. *Adequate rest* time between workouts is essential to promote physiological adaptation. Only infrequently are training gains greater by working the same muscle groups every day. Most athletes who work out every day concentrate on different aspects on alternate days. Nearly complete rest (allows loosening up only) for two to three days prior to a competition is now standard practice. This principle has obvious application to ski conditioning but it also emphasizes the importance of skiers being in shape before they "hit" the slopes, since then there is not adequate recovery time between participation "workouts." Ski lift tickets are too expensive to waste much time resting, and few can afford to take any whole days off even if muscles, joints, and systems are screaming for rest.

9. *Other training variables* can greatly influence the outcome of training. Among these variables are (1) intensity (how hard one works or pushes oneself), (2) frequency (how often you work out, (3) duration (how long the workout lasts), and (4) progressions (the way in which overloads are increased or progress is planned). Recommendations regarding these training variables are found throughout Sections 6 and 7.

10. *Interval training* is frequently tolerated better than continuous training, since it causes less "perceived strain" on the body, that is, the worker can get through the workout better by short periods of work followed by rest than if continuous work is performed. This is true even though the intensity of the work performed during each interval is usually greater than the intensity that could be performed at any time if done continuously (13). It makes sense for skiers to practice some interval training, since most downhill skiing is interval in nature, that is, periods of high-energy expenditure and performance are followed by periods of rest.

11. *Rapid retraining* or first-time training will not be tolerated by per-

sons who are in poor general, physical condition. It is better to progress slowly and allow time for both physiological and psychological adaptation to occur. For some reason, the second day after the first training session seems to produce the greatest amount of soreness and stiffness. Participants who enter training should expect this to occur, and they should plan to work slowly through this difficult period. There is little evidence that a pretraining conditioning period (very light activity) does much to alleviate the pains and soreness that occur following increases in work load or intensity, that is, when an individual trains at any level that exceeds their existing state of adaptation.

12. The *safest* type of training for older persons or those with hypertension or a previous history of heart disease is closely supervised activity involving the legs in slow (walk or jog, not run) dynamic, rhythmic movements. This type of activity promotes C-R fitness, with a minimal increase in heart rate and blood pressure. This principle emphasizes safety during training but also explains the reason why many elderly persons can continue skiing, that is, it can be viewed as a sport involving rhythmic, dynamic contractions of leg, trunk, and arm muscles and can be pursued at varying intensities during recreational participation.

13. Ligaments, tendons, and other connective tissues can be made *less stiff* by stretching exercises. This results in an increased flexibility and range of motion at stiffened joints. Furthermore, proper flexibility-extensibility training can forestall the development of joint and spinal stiffness that has become so "popular" in our contemporary society. We have included an extensive series of stretching-flexibility exercises in Section 7, p. 000 and a set of preski warmup exercises in Section 7, p.000.

As a final note on optimum training, it is important to mention that coaches who have recently utilized scientifically based coaching tenets while working with athletes have had remarkable success. This has implications for ski instructors who assist in devising training programs and for those who devise their own, since both should be structured in a scientific and intelligent manner. Today it is not good enough to recommend that students simply "train" or "workout" for their sport using a haphazard approach. This especially holds true, since the data on scientific approaches to training are accumulating so rapidly, and so much more is known today about how best to train or to optimally train than was known only 15 years ago. It is currently inadequate for an instructor, coach, or trainer to "tell" an athlete to perform a drill without explaining the "why" for doing it (especially if asked). Instructors who respond with, "do it this way because some champion does it" or because "that's the way I learned" or because "it's the best way," are frequently open to rebellious actions by their charges, mainly as a result of their sophisticated level of knowledge.

SECTION 6

A Case for Year-Round Physical Conditioning

WHY IT'S MOST IMPORTANT

The importance of maintaining a high level of general physical fitness between seasons cannot be overemphasized for skiers. In fact, the concept of seasons and preseason conditioning, for example, may in a way be self-defeating when contrasted to an alternative approach of participating in sports and staying in good condition all year. Using the year-round conditioning approach, a skier's overall, general physical fitness becomes the foundation on which special preseason conditioning preparations are made. Skiers who are already in good physical condition can approach their preseason exercises with optimism and enthusiasm, realizing that this is but a final stage of preparation to more fully enjoy a complete season of skiing. Here, some of the better documented benefits of participating in year-round programs to promote personal physical fitness will be defined along with a description of some special needs of skiers, as compared to other sports participants. This will be followed by some recommended workouts that skiers could follow to insure an improvement

53

or maintenance of their general physical fitness level on a year-round basis.

KNOWN ADAPTATIONS

It is well established that people who work out on a regular basis (sometimes called "chronic" exercisers) display physiological adaptations that set them apart from their more sedentary counterparts. These adaptations can be viewed as bodily changes that occur over a period of time and improve the individual's chances of survival because of improved capability of counteracting or coping with a variety of subsequent stresses. A most important underlying concept of adaptation is that the adaptations do not occur unless the body, or parts of it, are overloaded, taxed, stretched, or fatigued during workouts. Some of the better documented adaptations possessed by physically-fit individuals are listed below, followed by short definitions. These terms will be used repeatedly in subsequent sections, and the reader should be clear on the specific meaning of each. It is usually convenient to think of adaptations in terms of individuals possessing more or less of some characteristic than a nonadapted person. You should be aware that most of these contrasts are based on average values from experimental study groups and, because of large individual differences that can occur for any measurement variable, it is quite easy to identify "exceptions to the rule," that is, it is not difficult to recall someone who was sedentary most of their life yet retained a relatively strong body. Therefore, it should be helpful to think that, "on the average," chronically active people display certain beneficial adaptations that can take the form of more or less of something.

"More of" adaptations. In the case of these adaptations it can be added that physically-fit individuals have greater, improved, better, or increased measures of the particular characteristics.

1. Muscular strength—usually separated into dynamic and static strength, with dynamic meaning the maximum force that can be exerted by a group of muscles during limb or trunk movement (also called isotonic), while static denotes a force exerted against an immovable object (also called isometric).

2. Muscular endurance—the number of times a muscle group can lift a given load at a fixed cadence before fatiguing appreciably

(dynamic endurance), or the length of time a muscle group can exert a fixed force before fatiguing (static endurance).

3. Muscular power—a measure of the rate of force application or the maximum number of times a muscle group can lift a fixed load in a given period of time. The term relates best to dynamic work conditions, since power is defined as work per unit time. A similar measure for static muscle "power" might be the number of static exertions that can be made to a fixed level of force in a given period of time.

4. Connective tissue tensile and sheer strength—measures of the forces that tendons, ligaments, and cartilage can withstand before these tissues suffer compression or tearing damage; can be easily related to the concept of joint injury thresholds.

5. Neuromuscular reactions and reflexes—measures of the speed with which an individual can react to a stimulus or situation and make appropriate body or limb movements to correct balance, adjust center of gravity, coordinate movements, etc. Much of the adaptation here may reside in the muscular portion of the response system rather than in the neural portion.

6. Cardiorespiratory endurance—a measure of how long an individual can perform submaximal work tasks involving many large muscle groups (jogging, running, swimming, uphill walking, bike riding) before becoming exhausted. An indirect measure of the adapted state of the heart, lungs, muscle cells, and circulatory system.

7. Aerobic power on maximum oxygen consumption—a measure of the maximal capability of the body to utilize oxygen in the metabolism of fuel substrates (sugars and fats) to produce usable energy for muscle contraction and other essential functions during physical activity.

"Less of" adaptations. In the case of these adaptations, it can be said that physically-fit individuals have less, lower, reduced, or decreased measures of the particular characteristics.

1. Lower resting heart rate — also termed resting bradycardia of training. The resting heart rate may be 10 to 25 beats per minute slower. Normal resting rate is about 65 to 75 for men and 70 to 80 for women in the untrained state.

2. Decreased percentage of body fat and, conversely, a higher percentage of lean tissue. Both are important adaptations as related to health and physical performance.

3. Less muscle and joint soreness response to a vigorous workout.

4. Less spinal rigidity. Could be viewed as an improved extensibility, flexibility, and range of motion.

Now that we have identified some of the beneficial adaptations that go along with being physically fit, let us examine some of the special needs of skiers. Essentially, the question is, "What is so unique about this sport that we should be concerned about year-round and preseason conditioning?" A close look at skiing in contrast to many other sports indicates several differences that substantiate the need for special emphasis on conditioning.

Skiing is a seasonal sport, which frequently arrives overnight and catches enthusiasts with their "shape" down. Couple this with the fact that many skiers seldom "work into" the sport but attempt to participate at a level near the limits of their ability, and the result is a potential for trauma greater than that for other sports. Like some professional athletes, skiers are frequently in their peak of condition, perhaps still not very good, at the beginning of the season and deteriorate progressively thereafter. Much of this deterioration may be due to the infrequency of skiing since, although the average skier spends 14 days per year on the slopes, many of these days are crammed into long weekend ski outings.

There are still other differences between skiing and other sports in relation to protective gear and playing surfaces. Skiing is a high-velocity sport with hazards of falls and collisions with fixed obstacles or other skiers, yet little or no protective gear such as pads or helmets is worn. This seems unreasonable when you consider that it has been estimated that speeds ranging from 24 to 100 mph may be attained by a 190 pound skier in a medium crouch position on slopes ranging from 3 to 45 degrees (14). Although these speeds are calculated for optimum skiing conditions, skiers more often find themselves facing less than optimum conditions that present another hazard not found in most other sports. In skiing, the terrain and conditions are uncontrollable and constantly varying, that is, the skier can depend on no standardization of playing surface and cannot participate indoors with better control over environmental conditions.

To make our argument for year-round conditioning complete, we will now attempt to intelligently relate some of the known adaptations to the special needs of skiers. In some cases, the arguments are based on intuitive reason and prudent application instead of on "hard" science. This is an approach that must be taken when all of the facts are not available but one wishes to interpret these facts that are. For example, it seems reasonable that skiers who possess improved muscle strength, endurance, and power not only have the ability to perform better but can do so with relatively less fatigue. These abilities can have far-reaching implications for the self-protection of skiers because they can better initiate proper protective actions in surprise emergency situations. In addition, they may be capable of making more sound judgements and decisions in situations that depend on their muscular prowess because they know better the limits of their strength and endurance. A final advantage to good muscle conditioning is that little or no muscle and joint soreness occurs even after vigorous training sessions or during the first days on the slopes. This is a difficult adaptation for most weekend athletes to accept. We have personally experienced many first-of-the-season ski outings with no soreness while much younger but less conditioned skiers have moved stiffly around the lodge complaining of their many aches and pains. Unfortunately, this pain and suffering is a detraction from the enjoyable aspects of the weekend experience and could have been avoided by some preskiing conditioning.

Skiers who maintain faster neuromuscular reactions and reflexes will also be at an advantage in terms of both performance and self-preservation. During game situations, performers are constantly reacting to cues and, hopefully, selecting proper courses of action. The better skilled performers generally anticipate better, react more quickly, and display a better selection of response. It is reasonable to expect that skiers who have kept their neuromuscular systems in good condition during the "off-season" will be more ready to quickly anticipate a change in terrain, to correct their balance through sensitive reflex mechanism, to quickly elect the most favorable response and, if all else fails, be able to fall more gracefully and safely.

At this point, the reader might agree that skiers with well-conditioned muscles and neural systems would be at an advantage but might question how an improved cardiorespiratory endurance or aerobic power could have any application. A quick review of the definitions reveals that these measures are an indication of the body's ability to take in, circulate, and utilize oxygen for chemical conversion of energy from carbohydrates or fats to a form that can be used for muscle contraction and maintenance functions—ATP.

A skier who is in good physical condition will be able to perform the work of skiing utilizing aerobic metabolism for longer periods of time than a skier who is less fit. This means that a maximum number of ATP will be generated from either carbohydrate or fat-fuel substrates, and the individual will need to resort less to the anaerobic production of ATP. Since much less energy is derived anaerobically as opposed to aerobically, a skier with improved fitness is at a distinct advantage. The advantages that they enjoy show up in a variety of ways such as reduced perception of exertion, reduced rate of breathing, and the fact that when rest is necessary, it is due to localized muscle fatigue rather than a generalized feeling of exhaustion. Once again, it makes good sense for a skier to maintain a high level of cardio-respiratory endurance, since this can greatly add to his or her enjoyment of skiing.

The effects of year-round physical conditioning on adaptations that relate to the maintenance of spine and joint flexibility and extensibility, and to strong tendons and ligaments should not be passed over lightly. It is common practice to think of injuries to joints, tendons, and ligaments as being the result of deforming forces that have exceeded the "injury threshold levels" of these connective tissues. Since injury thresholds can be viewed as relating to both the strength of connective tissues and to their extensibility, it is also common to associate injury with tissues that have become stiff or joints that have become inflexible over the years. Since the strength of any muscle-bone-connective-tissue system is only as strong as the weakest link, it makes sense for skiers to maintain good joint flexibility, extensibility, and strength. If this is done, injury threshold levels will be maintained at a high level, and the potential for injury because of routine falls and accidents will be diminished. This could be the explanation for the serious injuries that some skiers incur when experiencing falls that would appear to be nontraumatic. In subsequent sections, the importance of flexibility and extensibility exercise will be emphasized along with the importance of improving muscular strength. The final advantages to being physically fit relate to skiing performance, personal appearance, and practicality. This is a matter of controlling body weight so that you do not develop excessive fatness between seasons. The advantages in terms of appearance are obvious and in terms of practicality are apparent. Skiers who maintain their body weight between seasons can utilize ski clothing from one season to the next, which has real, practical ramifications. Furthermore, they will have fewer problems with body control when skiing if excessive body weight in the form of fat does not have to be carried along. Since excessive fat deposits can make one top heavy, bottom heavy, or a combination of both and, consequently, slow down bodily movements and reactions, there is also an increased potential for injury because of loss of control.

In summary, we have outlined a multitude of physiological adaptations that are known to occur in physically-fit persons. Although the primary reason for maintaining a high level of fitness is additional enjoyment of the sport, skiers should be aware of the enjoyable aspects of other sports that they might engage in on a year-round basis. Participation in these other sports eventually means that there is no concept of a season but only a continuation of a series of seasons, each season opening the way to the beginning of a new and different sport, which is also enjoyable. Participation in these activities and the resulting maintainance of physical capabilities, without the detriment of pain, strain, and soreness, allows recreational athletes to function on an entirely different dimensional plane than their more sedentary neighbors. It only makes sense then to stay in shape on a year-round basis and to finish up your preparation for any particular sport with some preseason conditioning activities.

BEST METHODS TO ACHIEVE

Now that we have established a case for year-round physical conditioning, "What types of activities are best?" Most American College of Sports Medicine experts on this topic currently agree that physical activities that engage large muscle masses in rhythmic-dynamic movements of submaximal intensity, so that they can be endured for a considerable period of time, are best for stimulating adaptations in cardiorespiratory fitness. Among these activities are fast walking, jogging, running, bicycle riding, swimming of laps, and recreational games and sports, provided that they are vigorous and they are engaged in on a regular basis. It is further recommended that these activities be done a minimum of three times a week for periods lasting from 20 minutes to one and one-half hours.

The reader will note that 20 to 90 minutes represents a considerable time for activities to be pursued and might wonder how this can be so. The important concept here is that activities that are of high intensity do not have to be pursued for such long periods of time, that is, running two miles in 20 minutes can provide as much stimulus to maintaining physical fitness as participating in tennis for one and one-half hours. The key point and consideration is the matter of exercise or training intensity. For information on comparative energy costs and intensities of performing a variety of common physical activities, you are referred to "The New Aerobics," by Cooper (15).

One of the best activities for all-round physical conditioning is jogging and running. A minimum recommendation is that all people run two miles three times a week and attempt to complete the distance in 16 to 22 mintues. For those who want to quantify their workout intensities in terms of heart rate, they should either determine their maximum heart rate while at the point of voluntary exhaustion or they can estimate their age-related maximum heart rate using tabled values (16). Once maximum heart rate is known or estimated, you simply subtract your ordinary resting heart rate from that amount to yield a difference between resting and maximum heart rate levels. If you now take 70 to 80 percent of the difference and add this product to your resting rate, the sum represents a target heart rate that you should achieve during your jogging or running activity. Establish a pace that you can maintain for the entire two mile distance while your heart rate remains on target, that is, it does not exceed the established, target heart rate. If the target heart rate is exceeded, you should slow your pace until heart rate drops to the desired level. Following this type of procedure you will find, over a period of as little as two to three weeks, that your work performance is much improving, since you can complete the two mile distance in less time without exceeding your target heart rate values. These are all indications that you are becoming progressively more fit and that your cardiorespiratory system is adapting.

Since these recommended activities primarily involve use of the legs, they will do much for conditioning the lower part of the body but may be lacking in conditioning the upper body in terms of muscular strength, endurance, and flexibility. It is, therefore, advisable that sets of calisthenics or weight training activities be used to promote upper body fitness. Earlier, weight training was de-emphasized for the recreational athlete because it was thought that cardio-respiratory outcomes were the most desirable and a minimum level of strength and endurance would be a concommitant outcome. It is currently believed that, in the sedentary occupations at which most of us work, it is impossible to maintain upper body strength unless one practices weight training, calisthenics, or gymnastic-type activities.

The question is always raised about whether there is good transfer of skills from one activity to another and whether or not it would be particularly advantageous for skiers to practice one sport as opposed to another one during the off-season months. It is acknowledged that there is a good deal of carry-over between activities like water skiing and surfing to the sport of skiing. These sports require many of the same reactions to momentary losses of balance and shifts in center of gravity that are encountered in skiing, and they require good muscular endurance. Presumably, there is also considerable carry-over from sports where the benefits are not so apparent. For example, if people participate on a regular basis in volleyball, they are not only forced to react quickly to situations but frequently must extend their bodies into off-balance positions and then make adjustments and corrections or go into a fall or roll performed in a safe and noninjurious manner. The same would also be true for participation in a variety of recreational sports like soccer, football, basketball and, for that matter, hiking over rough terrain.

SECTION 7
Special Condi-
tioning Programs

Now that we have established that there are distinct phases to optimum training and scientifically based reasons for selecting certain exercises, depending on the desired specificity of outcome, let us define some "good" exercises for preseason conditioning, for maintenance training during the season, and for warm-up. Here, sets of exercises will be listed to include some where ski equipment such as poles and skies are used during the exercises. Other exercises will employ resistances provided by the entire body or its segments, by weight training apparatus, or by a buddy resistance system. Several of the exercises will emphasize stretching and flexibility development rather than increase in strength or endurance. In each case, the exercise will be described through the use of photographs showing the trainee in key positions during the execution of the exercise. Written descriptions will also provide the familiar and scientific names of the muscles involved, the action of these muscles, the specific training approach viewed as optimum, a short, general description of the exercise, and the number of recommended repetitions, ideas for progressions in intensity, and an indication of any hazardous aspects of the exercise.

Since a variety of training methods are suggested, it is essential that users understand the manner in which resistances are to be applied. Basically, the recommended exercises include isometric contractions, dynamic contractions with limb or trunk movement, and stretching-flexibility exercises.

Isometric contractions are made against, immovable objects—a wall; against self-applied resistance—hands and arms; against the neck; against noncompressible objects—a broomstick; or against a resistance provided by another person—buddy resistance. The principle behind this training dictates that there be no joint movement but that muscle-contractile tension be maximum. To be effective, this training requires concentration to insure that muscles are maximally contracted during the entire hold period. This is especially true for exercises where the individual self-applies the counterbalancing resistance, or when maximum contractions are made at the limits of joint range of motion. When buddy resistance is applied, it is important that the force applied is adequate enough to counter any movement by the performer.

Dynamic exercises are performed using either all or a portion of one's own body weight as the overload resistance and using contracting muscles so that limb or trunk movements result. In most cases, weights or buddy resistance are added to create more of an overload. If the amount of weight to be used is not specified, it can be determined through trial and error. It is safe to start with light loads and experiment with increasingly heavier ones to determine a manageable starting load. In cases where three sets of six repetitions are recommended, this would be a weight heavy enough so that it could barely be lifted during the sixth lift of each set. It is important to keep records of the amount of weight lifted for each exercise and add weight whenever possible. The amount of weight you can add varies greatly but may be 2½ to 5 pounds for dumbbells, 5 to 15 pounds for arm and shoulder exercises, and 15 to 25 pounds for leg and trunk exercises. When following systematic, progressive weight training, the amount of weight added should theoretically return the lifter to a performance level of three sets and six repetitions. This seldom works out exactly. In cases where a lifter is working alone, it is advisable to use lighter loads and avoid possible losses of balance that might occur without spotters. When buddy resistance is provided for dynamic movements, it is important that lifters be allowed to move their limbs through a full range of motion. Since the resistance buddies have mechanical advantage because of position or leverage, they can stop all movement but must not do so. Usually, the movement can be simply analyzed, and countering resistance can be applied throughout. If the movement is too fast, apply more resistance, if too slow, let up some. Verbal communication between buddies adds greatly to the effectiveness of these exercises.

The stretching and flexibility exercises are intended to promote improvements in the range of motion of both spine and limb joints. One technique to be used involves stretching to the limits of the joint with repeated movements but without a forceful bouncing motion that might induce unwanted strain. A second technique involves static stretching where the performer stretches to the limits of the joint, then goes just beyond this point (by one-half to one inch) and holds for a count of ten. These techniques will be referred to as dynamic and static techniques, respectively.

PRESEASON CONDITIONING

We have made a case earlier for the importance of year-round conditioning, but we realize that most people will enter the ski season in a state of poor physical fitness. The reasons for this condition will vary somewhat but will ultimately be resolved because regular participation in physical activity to maintain fitness has been relegated to a low priority status. In fact, a 1972 article (17) reveals that 85 percent of adult women and 50 percent of adult men may be "unfit" to pursue skiing. These percentages are from results of 3500 persons who performed the Kasch exercise test administered by YMCA personnel at four national ski shows. This is a three-minute step test where the performer steps up and down on a 12-inch step at a rate of 24 complete step cycles per minute. Judgements of cardiorespiratory fitness are based on how well the performer's heart rate recovers back toward resting levels when work is stopped. This pulse rate count is made during the first minute of recovery. A more complete description of this test is given in Section 8, p. 000, where consideration is given to preseason or initial evaluations. The majority of skiers will not be in good physical condition and should be encouraged to initiate programs of general physical fitness well in advance of the ski season. The rationale to this recommendation is that although the exercises defined later will assist in improving strength, flexibility, coordination, and endurance, they will not serve as a substitute for programs that promote a skier's general level of fitness and allow them to establish and maintain a high level of fitness between seasons. If skiers can be convinced of the importance of maintaining a high level of general physical fitness, more than half the battle has been won. Then, if a program of specific exercises is practiced for a period of two to four weeks prior to the first ski outing, skiers would perform better, enjoy their sport more, have less soreness, and be less prone to injury. This last point about injury proneness is made without statistical evidence— that skiers who have practiced preseason conditioning actually experience fewer injuries. Until the evidence is conclusive, it sometimes behooves us to follow a procedure that intuitively seems most prudent. As mentioned previously, one can argue forcefully for the increased ability of conditioned skiers to "correct themselves" out of potentially injurious situations and that the injury threshold of muscles, ligaments, and tendons can be improved through strengthening and stretching exercises.

EXERCISE NO. 1   ABDOMINAL CURL AND HOLD.

Muscles:	Abdominal region (Figure 1, No. 1); Rectus Abdominis.
Action:	Flexion of trunk.
Optimum Training:	Static endurance.
Execution:	Curl up one-half way and hold to 10 count, also curl up three-fourths way and hold to 10 count.
Progressions:	Use weights, incline board, increase hold time or buddy pressure.
Precautions:	Keep knees bent throughout to work abdominal muscles, and avoid excessive curvature and strain on lower back.

A. Start

B. One-Half way

C. Three-Fourths way

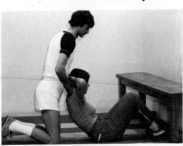

D. Buddy pressure

67

EXERCISE NO. 2   THIGH SQUEEZE.

Muscles: Inner thigh (groin) (Figure 2, No. 2 and Figure 4, No. 17); Many adductors.

Action: Keep thighs together.

Optimum training: Static endurance.

Execution: Press knees slowly outward to limits while resisting with thigh muscles. Repeat five times using 10 seconds per repetition.

Progressions: Increase repetitions to 10. Also squeeze pillow or beach ball following above hold times and repetitions.

Precautions: None.

A. Start

B. Midway
(5 sec)

C. Full
(10 sec)

D. Squeezing pillow

69

EXERCISE NO. 3   BUTTOCKS SQUEEZE AND HOLD.

Muscles:	Buttocks (Figure 2, No. 3); Gluteus Maximus.
Action:	Pelvic thrust.
Optimum training:	Dynamic strength and static endurance.
Execution:	Thrust pelvis forward by contracting buttocks fully, and hold for count of 10. Repeat five times.
Progressions:	Increase repetitions to 10. Also thrust pelvis forcefully against wall surface following above hold times and repetitions.
Precautions:	None.

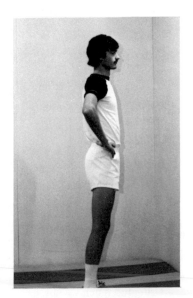

A. Start

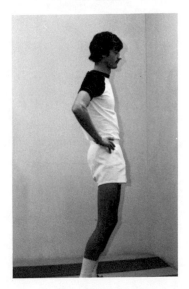

B. Thrust

71

EXERCISE NO. 4   THIGH EXTENSION AND HOLD.

Muscles: Back part of thigh (Figure 2, No. 4); Biceps
                     Femoris, Semitendinosus, Semimembranosus
                     (hamstrings).

Action: Assist pelvic thrust.

Optimum training: Static endurance.

Execution: Raise straightened leg to maximum up position
                     and hold for five count. Repeat 10 times for each
                     leg.

Progressions: Increase hold time to 10 seconds. Also use ankle
                     weights or buddy resistance following above
                     holding times and repetitions.

Precautions: Using too much weight.

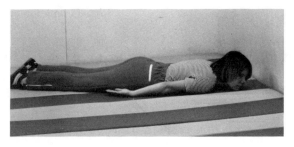

A. Start

B. Lift & hold

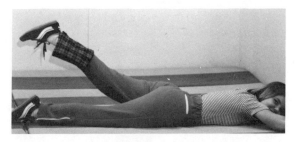

C. With weights

D. Buddy pressure

EXERCISE NO. 5   ANKLE ROLL-IN AND HOLD.

Muscles: Outside lower leg (Figure 2, No. 5); Peroneus
                     Longus.

Action: Rolling onto inside edges of feet.

Optimum training: Static endurance.

Execution: Roll slowly onto inside edges of feet and hold
                     for 10 count. Repeat five times.

Progressions: Increase repetitions to 10. Also against applica-
                     tion of downward pressure by buddy or while
                     holding weights.

Precautions: None.

A. Roll & hold

B. With weights

C. Buddy pressure

EXERCISE NO. 6   NECK EXTENSION AND HOLD.

Muscles: Back of neck (Figure 3, No. 6); Semispinalis
                        Capitis and Cervicis.

Action: Draw head back.

Optimum training: Static endurance.

Execution: Force head back to maximum position and hold
                        for 10 seconds. Repeat five times.

Progressions: Increase repetitions to 10. Also self-apply resist-
                        ance or weights at different positions follow-
                        ing above holding times and repetitions.

Precautions: Light-headed feeling after each hold. Relieved
                        by head-rolling action between exertions.

A. Head back and hold

B. Resistance applied

C. Harness & weights

EXERCISE NO. 7   SHOULDER EXTENSION.

Muscles: Shoulder and Chest (Figure 3, No. 7); Deltoids, Pectorals.

Action: Movement of upper arm forward and backward at shoulder.

Optimum training: Dynamic strength.

Execution: Drive fully extended arm downward and backward, and return to forward position with control. Repeat six times and do three sets.

Progressions: Increase repetitions to 10, then add weight and work up again from six repetitions.

Precautions: Failure to control weights on return to forward position.

A. Start

B. Finish

C. Start

D. Finish

EXERCISE NO. 8   ARM EXTENSION.

Muscles: Back part of upper arm (Figure 3, No. 8); tri-
                        ceps.

Action: Straighten arm at elbow.

Optimum training: Dynamic strength and endurance.

Execution: Start in down position and push up arms to
                        extended position. Do 15 "good" repetitions.

Progressions: Increase repetitions to 30. Women begin from
                        a position of knees in contact with floor rather
                        than toes (modified or executive pushup). Also
                        bench-press weights.

Precautions: None. False performance by not having body
                        straight or by doing incomplete pushups.

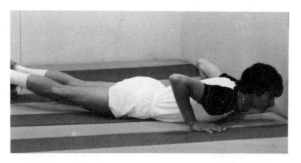

A. Start

B. Up position

C. Modified version

D. Bench-Press up position

81

EXERCISE NO. 9   HAND GRIP AND HOLD.

Muscles: Lower arm and hand (Figure 3, No. 9); Flexor Digitorum and Flexor Pollicis.

Action: Close hand and flexion at wrist.

Optimum training: Static strength and endurance.

Execution: Squeeze ¾ in. to 1 in. diameter noncompressible object (broomstick, tightly rolled and taped newspaper, or magazine) using flexed position with maximum effort to 10 count. Repeat five times with each hand.

Progressions: Increase repetitions to 10. Can also apply resistance with other hand and extend back slowly to a 10 count. Also use wrist machine.

Precautions: None. Must concentrate on applying flexion force during applied resistance.

A. Start

B. Squeeze-Flex position

C. Applying resistance

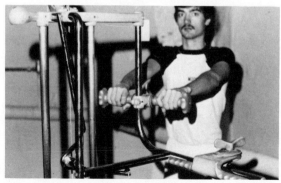

D. Wrist machine

83

EXERCISE NO. 10   ARM PULL-DOWN.

Muscles: Lateral aspects of back (Figure 3, No. 10); Latissimus Dorsi.

Action: Upper arm extension at shoulder.

Optimum training: Dynamic endurance.

Execution: Keeping arms straight, lift body from down to up position, or pull weighted bar from up position to down and return to up position with control. Repeat 20 times and do three sets.

Progressions: Increase to 30 repetitions, then add weight and work back up from 20.

Precautions: Failure to control weights on return to up position. Kneel on pads or mat to avoid sore knees. *A* and *B* must be done slowly using a straight, arm-lifting effort.

A. Start

B. Finish

C. Start

D. Finish

EXERCISE NO. 11   TRUNK RAISERS.

Muscles: Originate in lower back (Figure 3, No. 11); Sacro-
                      spinalis (erector spinae).

Action: Trunk extension.

Optimum training: Static endurance.

Execution: Raise trunk to up position and hold for five
                      count. Do 10 in straight-extension position and
                      10 with trunk rotation to the right and left.

Progressions: Increase hold to 10 count. Can also use hand-
                      held weights and buddy resistance.

Precautions: Raising up too vigorously. Causes undue strain
                      to lower back.

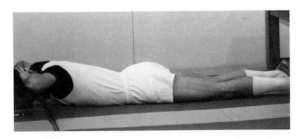

A. Start

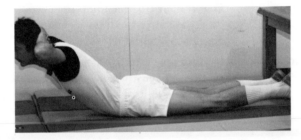

B. Up position

C. Up position with rotation

D. Buddy pressure

87

EXERCISE NO. 12   BODY LOWERING.

Muscles: Front portion of thighs (Figure 3, No. 12); Quadri-
                         ceps group.

Action: Extension and controlled flexion at knee.

Optimum training: Static strength and endurance.

Execution: Lower body to one-third and two-thirds knee-
                         bend position. Hold for count of 10 at each
                         position and repeat five times.

Progressions: Increase count to 20 at each position. Also use
                         weights or buddy pressure.

Precautions: Doing full knee bends without adequate condi-
                         tioning, feet slipping forward with loss of balance.

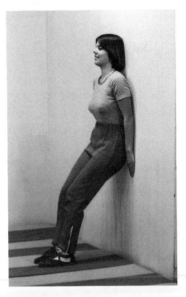

A. Start

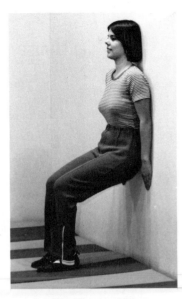

B. One-Third position

C. Two-Thirds position with
weights

D. Buddy pressure

EXERCISE NO. 13   JUMPING.

Muscles: Front portion of thighs and back of lower leg
                     (Figure 3, No. 12, No. 13 and Figure 4, No. 19);
                     Quadriceps group, Gastrocnemius.

Action: Explosive extension of legs and controlled land-
                     ing.

Optimum training: Dynamic strength and endurance.

Execution: With feet together, jump over obstacle (box,
                     pillow, books, etc.) from one side to the other
                     and back. Repeat 10 times, and do three sets
                     with rest between.

Progressions: Increase height of obstacle to 16 in. maximum,
                     and increase repetitions to 20 per set.

Precautions: Losing balance or catching a foot on obstacle,
                     especially when fatiguing. Use low, soft obstacles
                     at first.

A. Start

B. Midway

C. Completed

91

EXERCISE NO. 14   LEG EXTENSIONS.

Muscles: Front portion of thighs (Figure 3, No. 12 and Figure 4, No. 19); Quadriceps group.

Action: Leg extension against resistance.

Optimum training: Dynamic strength.

Execution: Press foot pedals forward as far as possible, and return slowly with control over weights. Do three sets with six repetitions per set.

Progressions: Increase to 10 repetitions then add weights and work back up from 6 repetitions. Also use buddy resistance.

Precautions: Failure to control weights on return position resulting in rapid flexion of knees and banging of weights.

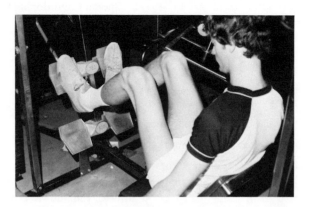

A. Start

B. Complete extension

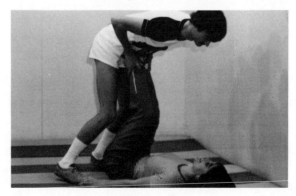

C. Buddy pressure

93

EXERCISE NO. 15   FOOT EXTENSION.

Muscles: Back part of lower leg (Figure 3, No. 13); Gastroc-
                      nemius.

Action: Rising onto toes.

Optimum training: Static endurance and stretching.

Execution: Position toes on 2 in. block and rise to full,
                      up position, hold for five count while maintain-
                      ing balance. Return to full, down position for
                      five count to stretch muscles. Do 10 repetitions.

Progressions: Increase hold count to 10 at each position and
                      use 4 inch block. Also work against weights or
                      resistance from buddy.

Precautions: Very forceful contraction or bouncing on return
                      resulting in excessive strain on Achilles tendons.

A. Start

B. Up position

C. Against weights

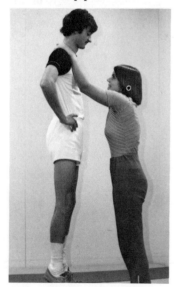

D. Buddy pressure

EXERCISE NO. 16   TRUNK LATERAL FLEXION.

Muscles: Deep lower back (Figure 4, No. 14); Quadratus
                         Lumborum.

Action: Bending upper body to side.

Optimum training: Dynamic strength and static endurance.

Execution: With barbell on shoulders, bend fully to one
                         side and hold for five count, return to upright
                         position and then bend to opposite side. Do
                         10 repetitions to each side using barbell equal
                         to one-fourth to one-third of body weight. In
                         A, raise trunk laterally from floor.

Progressions: Increase hold time to 10 count, and increase
                         weight of barbell. Also use buddy resistance.

Precautions: Loss of balance when bending to side; safer
                         to do with assistant.

A. Raise trunk

B. Start

C. Left hold position

D. Buddy pressure

EXERCISE NO. 17   TRUNK ROTATION.

Muscles: Along sides of spine (Figure 4, No. 15); sacro-
                        spinalis.

Action: Turning (rotating) upper body.

Optimum training: Dynamic strength and static endurance.

Execution: With barbell on shoulders, rotate trunk to full-
                        turn position and hold for five count. Return
                        to straight-ahead position, and rotate in opposite
                        direction. Do 10 repetitions to each side using
                        barbell equal to one-third to one-half of body
                        weight.

Progressions: Increase hold time to 10 count, and increase
                        weight on barbell. Also apply buddy resistance.

Precautions: Loss of balance because of weight of barbell.

A. Start

B. Rotate left

C. Buddy pressure

EXERCISE NO. 18   ABDOMINAL SIDE CURL.

Muscles: Middle and sides of abdomen (Figure 4, No. 16); Internal and External Obliques, Rectus Abdominis.

Action: Trunk flexion and rotation.

Optimum training: Static strength.

Execution: Curl and rotate to up position with left elbow inside right thigh. Strain against thigh for five count. Return to start position and repeat to opposite side. Do 10 to each side.

Progressions: Increase hold count to 10 seconds; use incline board or buddy pressure.

Precautions: Keep knees bent throughout as with exercise No. 1.

A. Start

B. Side curl right

C. Buddy pressure

101

EXERCISE NO. 19   LATERAL LEG LIFT.

Muscles: Deep abductor muscles of hip (Figure 4, No. 17);
                      Gluteus Medius and Minimus.

Action: Draw leg away at the hip.

Optimum training: Dynamic strength and static endurance.

Execution: Raise straightened leg to maximum up position
                      (abducted), and hold for five count. Repeat 10
                      times for each leg.

Progressions: Increase hold time to 10 seconds. Also use ankle
                      weights or buddy resistance following above
                      holding times and repetitions.

Precautions: Using too much weight.

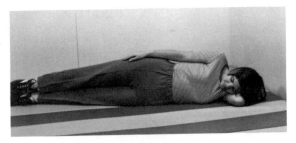

A. Start

B. Left leg raise

C. With weights

D. Buddy pressure

103

EXERCISE NO. 20   LEG ROTATION.

Muscles: Deep muscles of hip (Figure 4, No. 18); Six
                     outward rotators, and inward rotators (Gluteus
                     Medius and Minimus).

Action: Rotate leg at hip.

Optimum training: Dynamic strength.

Execution: Rotate leg outward, then inward against reverse
                     resistance or immovable object. Repeat 10 times
                     each direction for each leg.

Progressions: Apply more resistance while still allowing move-
                     ment.

Precautions: Pain to foot with improper holding.

A. Blocking-Right inward rotation

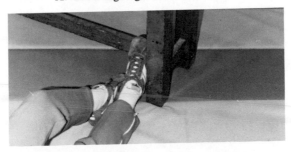

B. Blocking-Right outward rotation

C. Proper hold-right inward rotation

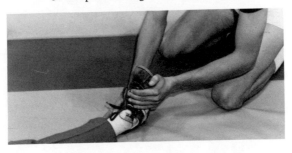

D. Proper hold-right outward rotation

EXERCISE NO. 21   KNEE FLEXION.

Muscles: Back portion of thigh (Figure 4, No. 19); Hamstrings.

Action: Bending of leg at knee.

Optimum training: Dynamic strength and endurance.

Execution: Pull leg through full range of motion against resistance. Do 10 repetitions with each leg.

Progressions: Apply more resistance while still allowing movement. Can also use weights.

Precautions: Tendency for cramping in full-flexion position; straighten out and rest before resuming.

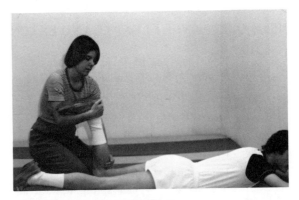

A. Start

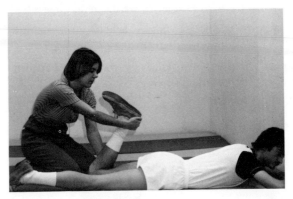

B. Full flexion position

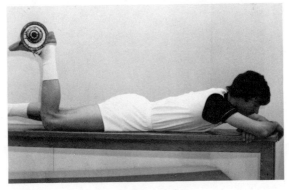

C. Using weights

107

EXERCISE NO. 22   KNEE FLEXION AND EXTENSION.

Muscles: Front portion of thighs and back of lower leg (Figure 4, No. 19 and Figure 3, No. 12); Quadriceps group, Gastrocnemius.

Action: Lowering of body and explosive extension of legs.

Optimum training: Dynamic strength and endurance.

Execution: Lower body from half-knee bend position with one leg back. Then spring upward and change position of legs while in air. Repeat 10 times with each leg forward and do three sets.

Progressions: Interlace fingers behind head, increase number of repetitions to 20, or use weights.

Precautions: Strain to knees by going to lower than half-knee bend position.

A. Half knee bend

B. Spring up

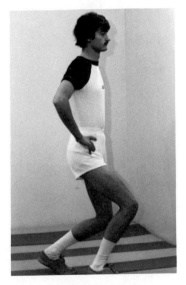

C. Change & land

D. With weights

EXERCISE NO. 23   ANKLE ROLL-OUT AND HOLD.

Muscles: Front and deep in back of lower leg (Figure 4, No. 20); Tibialis Anterior and Tibialis Posterior.

Action: Rolling onto outside edges of feet.

Optimum-training: Static endurance.

Execution: Roll slowly onto outside edges of feet and hold for 10 count. Repeat five times.

Progressions: Increase repetitions to 10. Also against application of downward pressure by buddy or while holding weights.

Precautions: None.

A. Roll and hold

B. With weights

C. Buddy pressure

EXERCISE NO. 24   CHEST-SHOULDER STRETCH.

Region stretched: Chest, shoulders, lateral back (Latissimus).

Execution: Extend arms and draw forward, back, down,
                           overhead, in intermediate planes, and describe
                           large circles so all muscles of shoulder girdle
                           are stretched. Use 15 dynamic-stretch move-
                           ments for each direction or static stretching
                           for a 10 to 15 count. For full effect, arms
                           should be crossed in forward, stretching posi-
                           tions.

Alternative positions: Standing, back-lying, seated, forward bend.
                           Can include head rolling and stretching from
                           standing and seated positions.

Precautions: Occasional dizziness with head rolling.

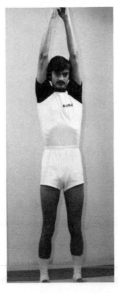

A. Standing arms overhead   B. Back lying arms crossed

C. Seated arms back

D. Forward bend

EXERCISE NO. 25   ABDOMINAL STRETCH.

Region stretched: Abdominal, front neck muscles.

Execution: Arch head or trunk into hyperextension posi-
                         tion. Apply stretch through either 15 dynamic-
                         stretch movements or static stretching for
                         a 10 to 15 count. Relax by lying flat between
                         each of three sets.

Alternative positions: Shoulder-feet, lying-arm support, "rocking."

Precautions: Avoid vigorous rocking. Persons with a history
                         of low-back pain should progress cautiously.

A. Shoulder-Feet position

B. Lying arm support position

C. Rocking

EXERCISE NO. 26   STRAIGHT LEG STRETCH-REACH.

Region stretched: Upper spine, shoulders, lower back and hamstrings.

Execution: Keeping legs together and as straight as possible, extend arms and stretch toward ankles and toes using either 15 dynamic-stretch movements or static stretching for a 10 to 15 count. Relax by twisting at hips between each of three sets.

Alternative positions: Standing, seated on floor with legs together, seated on floor with legs separated.

Precautions: Avoid excessive bounce during dynamic stretching.

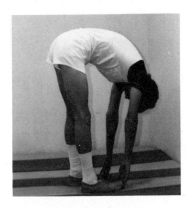

A. Standing

B. Seated legs together

C. Seated legs separated
Side stretch

D. Seated-Legs separated
forward stretch

117

EXERCISE NO. 27   KNEE-TO-CHEST STRETCH.

Region stretched: Lower back, buttocks, quadriceps, and upper spine in knee and shoulder positions.

Execution: Bring knee(s) to chest and grasp with arms. Pull in tightly using either 15 dynamic-stretch movements or static stretching for a 10 to 15 count. Relax by lying flat on back or abdomen between each of three sets.

Alternative positions: On side or back bringing one or both knees to chest. On knees or shoulders bringing both knees to chest.

Precautions: Avoid excessive bounce during dynamic stretching. Roll gently into shoulder position, and don't exert excessive static force on thighs with arms.

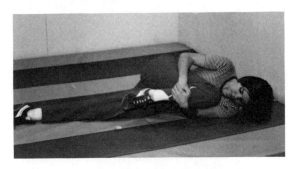

A. On side-one knee up

B. On back both knees up

C. On knees fetal position

D. On shoulders knees at head

EXERCISE NO. 28   LATERAL TRUNK STRETCH.

Region stretched: Sides of trunk.

Execution: Extend arm overhead and, without leaning
                           forward, bend from the waist as far as possible
                           to the side. When limits are reached, use 15
                           dynamic-stretch movements or static stretch-
                           ing for a 10 to 15 count. Relax by rotating
                           trunk back and forth between three sets in
                           each direction.

Alternative positions: Standing, seated on bench, seated on floor.

Precautions: Avoid excessive bouncing during dynamic
                          stretching.

A. Standing   B. Seated on bench

C. Seated on floor

EXERCISE NO. 29   GROIN AND HIP STRETCH.

Region stretched:

Adductors of inner thigh-groin region and outer region of lower leg. Abductors of hip with *C*.

Execution:

Place pressure on knees and thighs using elbows and upper-body weight. Grasp feet over instep and align soles of feet. Use 15 dynamic-stretch movements or static stretching for a 10 to 15 count. Relax by extending legs between each of three sets. For *C*, cross one leg over and hold, then do other leg.

Alternative positions: Yoga lotus.

Precautions:

Avoid excessive pressure during dynamic stretching. Work gradually toward full lotus position.

A. Seated

B. Lotus position

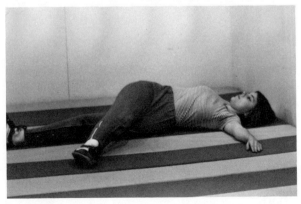

C. Hip stretch

123

EXERCISE NO. 30   THIG-ANKLE STRETCH.

Region stretched: Quadriceps, foot flexors on front of lower leg. Some calf and Achilles in forward-lunge position.

Execution: Stretch muscles by either grasping foot at instep or forcing downward with instep against floor. Do either 15 dynamic-stretch movements or static stretching for a 10 to 15 count. Relax while stretching other leg and do three sets for each leg.

Alternative positions: Standing, kneeling, and forward lunge.

Precautions: Avoid excessive bounce during dynamic stretching and excessive, backward lean in kneeling position until well-conditioned.

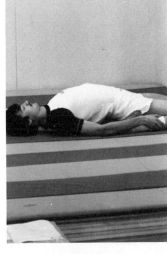

A. Standing   B. Kneeling

C. Forward lunge

EXERCISE NO. 31   CALF-ACHILLES STRETCH.

Region stretched: Back of lower leg and heel tendon.

Execution: Walk slowly away from wall or support while keeping heels flat on floor. When limits are reached, use 15 dynamic-stretch movements or static stretching for a 10 to 15 count. Relax by forcefully extending each foot between each of three sets.

Alternative positions: Standing, lowering to down position and relaxed extension.

Precautions: Avoid excessive bouncing during dynamic stretching. Proceed cautiously if Achilles-tendon pain occurs.

A. Standing

B. Lowering on block

C. Relax extension

MAINTENANCE DURING THE SEASON

A word of caution here! You have practiced your aerobic and preseason exercises diligently and you feel great; you skied better during your first outing and had fewer (if any) aches and pains. Now you're into full swing of the season and plan to ski every weekend and at least one weekday if you can get off work just a little early. Unfortunately, it doesn't work that way for most, and the 14 days a year spent on the slopes by the average skier are crammed into a few long, intense ski weekends. The result is the same as that experienced by professional athletes who are in peak condition at the start of the season, but show progressive decline thereafter. It seems that the weekly "games" are not adequate enough to promote retention of the adaptations you have worked so hard to acquire.

The simple solution to this is to continue to workout at home or in a gym even though you are also skiing. Plan these sessions so that you work out a minimum of once every three days (skiing counts as a workout).

Once you are in shape, both the duration and frequency of workouts can be reduced, and you can still maintain good, general physical fitness. Note that the term intensity was not mentioned. At this point, you are familiar with the exercises you have elected to do and can move efficiently from one to the other. Although you won't need to work out as long each session, continue to push yourself while doing each exercise so that the intensity of your total workout will be adequate. Be sure to continue you jogging or other areobic involvement.

During maintenance training, you can also cut back on the number of different exercises you do each session. Continue to concentrate on your individual weaknesses and do some work for those areas without fail. Also consider setting up two or three different workouts with 8 to 10 exercises included in each. Once again, choose exercises that allow for some conditioning and stretching, some static and dynamic work, and some work for various regions of the body. You can likely do this best by selecting exercises from Figure 5 and listing them on notecards. Exercises to correct weaknesses should be included in each workout plan. The inclusion of fewer exercises should allow aerobic activity to be performed during the same workout without it becoming too lengthly. Rigid adherence to these schedules along with a reasonable amount of skiing should insure maintenance of top conditioning throughout the ski season.

PRESKIING WARM-UP

The concept that skiers should perform warm-up exercises before they begin skiing has been best promoted by Tage Pedersen, official trainer for recent United States olympic ski teams.

Although competitive skiers may spend 30 to 45 minutes warming up for their events, it has not yet become "fashionable" for the recreational skier to perform warm-up exercises. Many skiers will ride four or more hours in an automobile, unload, don their gear, and go immediately to the slope they had "recently" mastered on their last outing—all without any formal warm-up; As a result, skiers may find themselves in difficult and hazardous situations without proper feelings of readiness to cope with them. This just doesn't make good sense! How many athletes in any sport, whether amateur, recreational, or professional, do you see going into full action before they have adequately warmed up, especially if ambient conditions are cold or the participant has been inactive for a considerable period? A likely answer is few or none.

As discussed in Section 4, p. 00, the matter of readiness, that is, the point when athletes consider that they are warmed up and ready, may have both physiological and psychological components. The importance of warming up properly should be emphasized in preseason conditioning workshops and demonstrations. If more skiers begin to practice warm-up exercises, then it becomes "fashionable" or the proper thing to do. To be more acceptable, it seems reasonable that they should be done on skis and while holding ski poles. The exercises should meet other criteria of emphasizing stretching and vigorous movement, and they should mimic the actions or positions encountered during subsequent activity. The cold, ambient conditions to which many skiers are exposed (especially beginners during lessons) may make it necessary to have an initial, general warm-up followed by maintenance warm-up at frequent intervals.

Several warm-up exercises that meet the above criteria are presented in subsequent photographs and descriptions. It is recommended that short bouts of all of the exercises be performed before starting to ski. One inherent danger in performing exercises where ski poles are grasped and moved during the exercise is injury to others from the sharp tips. Small children should not be permitted to do these exercises in congested areas, and adults should be wary. A rule that works well in golf and baseball where equipment is swung to warm up is that, while all parties should be cautious, primary responsibility resides with those who are passing by but not engaged in warm-up. The individual who is warming up may not see you during one action but may club you on the return movement. Caution—don't get too close to someone who is warming up!!

EXERCISE NO. 32   TRUNK-BEND TWIST.

Area emphasized: Trunk, back, shoulders.

Execution: With skis about shoulder width apart and ski poles behind neck with arms draped over ends, bend and twist trunk as shown. Do 5 to 10 movements in each plane.

Precautions: Avoid injury to others with pole tips.

A. Trunk twist

B. Side bending

C. Forward-bend twist

EXERCISE NO. 33   TOE TOUCHING.

Area emphasized: Lower back, hamstrings, shoulders.

Execution: Holding poles, with skis spaced as shown, bend down and touch instep or toes. Return to full, upright position with arms extended overhead between each of 10 touch movements.

Precautions: Avoid injury to others with pole tips.

A. Skis together forward touch

B. Skis apart twist touch

EXERCISE NO. 34   SIT BACK—ARMS EXTENDED.

Area emphasized: Abdominal, thighs, some lower leg.

Execution: With skis shoulder width apart, lower buttocks to bent-knee position. From there, bounce up and down several times. Do two to three repetitions.

Precautions: Avoid injury to others with pole tips, and don't bounce too vigorously during first set.

A. Bent knee (side)

B. Bent knee (front)

135

EXERCISE NO. 35   STATIONARY SLIDING AND
JUMPING.

Area emphasized: General warm-up, hips, legs.

Execution: With poles planted as shown and skis close together, slide feet back and forth while retaining same, general body position. Do three sets of 10 movements per leg, using a longer sliding action for each set. For jumps, keep feet together and spring upward, tucking knees so ski tips stay down but tails are moved progressively, first to one side and then back to the other. Do 15 total jumps.

Precautions: Be sure poles are properly positioned to the side and front of feet.

A. Stationary sliding

B. Stationary jumping

137

EXERCISE NO. 36   TRUNK ARCH AND HULA.

Area emphasized: Abdominal, back, hips, legs.

Execution: With skis close together and poles planted forward and outside of feet, arch trunk backward and return. Do 5 to 10 repetitions. Also, keep head stationary, and perform hula action by swinging hips and rolling onto ski edges. Do for count of 10 in each direction.

Precautions: Plant poles to assist with balance if arching back vigorously.

A. Back arch

B. Hula and edging
(front)

C. Hula and edging (side)

EXERCISE NO. 37   KNEE LIFTING.

Area emphasized: Knee, hip and spine.

Execution: With skis about six inches apart and poles planted outside and in front of toes, raise one knee toward chest as far as possible while also bending forward. Do five lifts with each leg.

Precautions: Plant poles firmly to assist with balance.

A. Right knee lift

Now that we have identified a considerable number of conditioning and stretching exercises that can be specifically related to skiing, an important question arises: Should all or just some exercises be performed? The reasonable answer is that one should consider the specific weaknesses of each individual and spend a majority of time in overcoming them. One of the best indicators of these weaknesses would be the location of isolated muscle fatigue while skiing or an inability to hold or repeat any particular skiing skill. A second indicator would be the location of minor and major strains and muscle soreness either during or a day or two after a strenuous outing on the slopes. After all, these aching joints and muscles are trying to tell you something about your lack of conditioning, and you should take heed.

Another approach that works well is to try all of the exercises and then list out a tailor-made program that covers all major muscle groups. If two or more exercises are given for the same muscle group and type of training (be heads up on this point), you may elect to perform only one or to alternate using some of the others. This alternation approach will add some variety to your workouts that might make them more interesting. Two examples of exercise programs that provide variety, yet cover major needs, are given below in Figure 5. The first program is an individual one that can be performed in a home setting (living room, recreation room, basement, or bedroom) without a need for other participants or special equipment. The second program requires weight-training equipment and a partner for the buddy exercises. This program might better be carried out in a weight-training room or health club. A person who followed either program in a systematic manner, that is, did the exercises on a regular basis, "pushed" themselves to improve, and maintained simple progress records would show dramatic improvements in as little as two weeks and much improvement by the end of the first month. Either of these programs would require between 45 minutes to one hour for completion, allowing some rest time between repetitions and exercises. Note that the exercises are ordered so that different muscle groups are worked, then rested, while others are worked. Recovery periods after performing exercises that cause localized fatigue can be used for stretching. The exercises listed in each program could be split into two sessions and performed on alternate days if this proved more convenient for people who work out each day and want to include some jogging or other areobic, cardiorespiratory fitness activity.

Remember, these programs are simply suggestions, and you should work to define your own special, optimum training program, that is, one that best meets your special needs. Since you should now understand the basic anatomical and optimum training considerations, you can operate on a do-it-yourself basis and be your own coach. If you have questions, contact a National Ski Patrol member who has received special training in conducting preseason conditioning workshops, a faculty member of your local school Physical Education department, or personnel at a YMCA or athletic club. These professionals are usually more than willing to provide consultory services. Although they will frequently provide service on a friendly, no-charge basis, you should be prepared to pay a professional fee for their services if they request it. If no fee is requested, it is becoming common practice to offer them a gratuity for their time and consultatory service, especially if it involves much time or repeated consultation.

EXERCISE NAME	GENERAL BODY REGION	EXERCISE NUMBER AND PAGE	
		HOME	GYM
Knee flexion and extension	Thighs	22 ABC p. 109	22 D p. 109
Neck extension and hold	Neck	6 B p. 77	6 C p. 77
Straight-leg Stretch-reach	Lower spine	26 ABC or D p. 117	26 ABC or D p. 117
Chest-shoulder stretch	Shoulders and arms	24 ABCD p. 113	24 ABCD p. 113
Body lowering	Thighs	12 AB p. 89	12 C or D p. 89
Knee to chest stretch	Upper spine	27 D p. 119	27 D p. 119
Thigh squeeze	Groin	2 ABC p. 69	2 D p. 69
Abdominal stretch	Abdomen	25 AB or C p. 115	25 AB or C p. 115
Ankle roll-in and hold	Lower leg	5 AB p. 75	5 C p. 75
Knee to chest stretch	Lower spine	27 ABC or D p. 119	27 ABC or D p. 119
Hand grip and hold	Arms and Hands	9 AB or C p. 83	9 D p. 83
Thigh-ankle stretch	Thigh and Lower leg	30 AB or C p. 125	30 AB or C p. 125
Trunk raisers	Lower back	11 AB or C p. 87	11 D p. 87
Calf-Achilles stretch	Calf and Achilles	31 A or B p. 127	31 A or B p. 127
Lateral leg lift	Hip	19 AB p. 103	19 C or D p. 103
Arm extension	Arms	8 AB or C p. 81	8 D p. 81
Groin and hip stretch	Groin	29 A or B p. 123	29 A or B p. 123
Thigh extension and hold	Buttocks	4 AB p. 73	4 C or D p. 73
Abdominal curl and hold	Abdomen	1 ABC p. 67	1 D p. 67
Ankle roll-out and hold	Lower leg	23 A p. 111	23 B or C p. 111
Shoulder extension	Shoulder-chest	7 AB p. 79	7 CD p. 79

Lateral trunk stretch	Trunk	28 AB or C p. 121	28 AB or C p. 121
Jumping	Legs	13 ABC p. 91	13 ABC p. 91
Abdominal side curl	Trunk	18 AB or C p. 101	18 AB or C p. 101
Foot extension	Calf and Achilles	15 A or B p. 95	15 C or D p. 95
Groin and hip stretch	Hip	29 C p. 123	29 C p. 123
Arm pull-down	Back and shoulders	10 AB p. 85	10 CD p. 85
Trunk lateral flexion	Trunk	16 A p. 97	16 BC or D p. 97
Buttocks squeeze and hold	Buttocks	3 AB p. 71	3 AB p. 71
Leg rotation	Hip	20 AB p. 105	20 CD p. 105
Knee flexion	Thighs	— —	21 AB or C p. 107

FIGURE 5. Example exercise programs for home and gymnasium settings.

SECTION 8
Conducting the Training Workshop

Advance planning is the key to organizing and conducting good workshops or training sessions, regardless of whether they are intended for skiers in general or for other instructors. Knowing, in advance, what material is to be covered, which exercises are going to be taught, how they can most effectively be presented, and why they should be emphasized is crucial. Consideration must also be given to questions of when (best time relative to start of ski season, vacations, etc.), where (adequate and convenient facility), and who will likely be attracted (age, sex, level of skiing experience). Facilities must be scheduled well in advance and written verification of the reservation obtained. Finally, consideration must be given to special equipment that is needed (slide projector, beach balls, weights, pillows, etc.) so it can be obtained several days in advance. If these and other details are observed, a much needed service will be provided for skiers that heretofore has been inadequate or completely lacking. In the following sections, we will look into some of these organizational and administrative matters in more detail.

147

INITIAL EVALUATION

There is some inherent danger in leading exercise sessions when the health and physical fitness status of individuals within the group are unknown. The danger is that some people may overexert themselves in an attempt to keep up with the group or to do exercises in the exact manner and quantity "demanded" by the leader as being good for all participants. These dangers can be considerably reduced by intelligent planning, in some cases through preliminary evaluations, and in all cases by judicious leadership.

Obtaining more information on paper about the group is an important first step to gaining insights into potential problems. Workshop application forms should request information about sex, age, height, current body weight, and previous injuries or current illnesses and disabilities. Applicants should be requested to make judgements about their current level of physical fitness and to give quantitative responses to questions of how often (times per week, month) they work out, how intensely (percent of maximum), and also what types of activities they do during workouts. Questions on whether applicants have ever been told by a medical practitioner that they currently have or previously have had high blood pressure, spinal problems, or diseases of their heart, lungs, or blood vessels should also be included. These should be accompanied by questions about prescription drugs they may be taking and whether or not they are heavy tobacco smokers. Figure 6 provides an example of brief medical history questions that might be included on a workshop application.

The above data can be used to good advantage provided that there is adequate time to review applications. Workshop announcements and application blanks should be sent out two to three months in advance, and a reasonable deadline should be set for returns. This deadline could be set three to four weeks before the workshop and should allow enough time to "screen" applicants whose responses may signal problems.

What does one look for on an application that may indicate that an applicant represents an elevated risk in terms of participating in supervised, strenuous exercises within a group setting? Check ages first and list those applicants separately who are between 35 and 45 years old and those older than 45. Note now that some recommendations regarding suggested versus required physical evaluations will

be given later. Next review body weights, particularly as they relate
to height. Extremely fat applicants can present problems during exercise participation and should be identified. These applicants are easy
to identify if you take a closer look at the heights of any males who
weigh over 190 pounds and any females weighing over 150 pounds.
Unless the males are taller that 5 feet and 10 inches and the females
taller than 5 feet and 7 inches, they are most likely carrying too much
fat. The amount of fat will, of course, vary considerably depending
on frame and musculature, and it will be greater in heavier or shorter
people when these arbitrary, fixed height-and-weight reference
standards are applied. The idea here is only to identify those who
represent potentially elevated risks because of fatness rather than
to precisely categorize all applicants on the basis of their body
fat.

After listing older applicants and identifying any who appear on
paper to be excessively fat, next review the injury, disability, and disease data to determine which applicants have experienced these problems. Recent injuries or current disabilities may require some special
planning and modification of program on the part of the leader. Those
applicants who indicate a presence or history of heart, vessel, or lung
disease must be identified and given some special consideration. The
same is true for persons with a history of chronic low-back pain or
spinal disease. In many cases, these applicants will be using medicinal
drugs to manage their condition, and such responses on the applications should also be noted. Finally, those individuals who, by their
own admission, have been extremely sedentary, perhaps having not
worked out regularly during the past several months, must be identified.

The reasons for identifying people through application questions
who present a higher than normal exercise-injury risk are clear. The
first concern is for the health and safety of the participants. A second
but, nonetheless, important concern is the matter of litigation that
could result from negligence or nonjudicious exercise leadership. This
raises the question then of what precautions should be taken in handling presumably high-risk people who have applied to participate
in the exercise workshop. Should they be told that they can not participate, which might cause undue alarm and also represent a gross
evaluation error, or should they be better classified into risk categories with more screening required dependent on their assigned risk

Application—Questionnaire
Ski-Conditioning Workshop
Sponsor—Mt. Holly National Ski Patrol

Name _____ Sex _____

Street Address _____ Age _____

City _____ State _____ Weight _____

Zip _____ Phone _____ Height _____

Describe ski experience _____ (Below, x one level)

_____ Beginner

_____ Intermediate

_____ Advanced

Describe physical fitness level . . . . (Below, x one level)

_____ Low

How often do you work out? _____ Average

How intensely do you work out? _____ High

What types of activities? _____

Describe any previous injuries and current disabilities to

joints or muscles _____

(Below, x one)

None _____

Some _____

Many _____

Brief Medical History

Date of last physical exam _____

Have you had any type of heart disease?   No _____ Yes _____

Any major illnesses in the past six months?   No _____ Yes _____

Do you experience any   Chest pain?   No _____ Yes _____

while climbing stairs   Breath shortness?   No _____ Yes _____

or exercising?   Light headed?   No _____ Yes _____

Do you have high blood pressure?   No _____ Yes _____

Do you have lung disease?   No _____ Yes _____

Do you have spinal problems (low-back pain)?   No _____ Yes _____

Are you taking prescribed drugs?   No _____ Yes _____

Do you smoke cigarettes?   No _____ Yes _____

Note. If answer to any of above questions is yes, then describe in more detail

_____

FIGURE 6. Example of workshop application-questionnaire to obtain important screening and assignment information (age, weight versus height, handicaps, physical fitness and medical history).

category? We think the latter approach is most sensible in contemporary society.

Applicants might reasonably be categorized into low-, moderate-, and high-risk groups as follows:

Low Risk. This group includes the majority of people who will apply — persons under 35 years of age of either sex who are not excessively obese and who indicate that they have been and are currently healthy. Applicants placed in this group will have been at least somewhat active during the past several months, most likely participating in a variety of recreational or competitive athletics. Members of this group should sign a statement that they are aware that they will be participating in vigorous, physical activity on a purely voluntary basis, that they are under no obligation to work beyond their individual capacity or to the point of exhaustion, or to do the activities in only the manner described or demonstrated. They should also indicate that they are reasonably able to participate in all activities without risk to their personal, long-term health or safety, although they will probably experience local muscle fatigue during participation and residual muscle and joint soreness lasting an indeterminant length of time after participation in the exercises. These disclaimer statements can be sent to applicants in this category as soon as they are indentified, with a request for immediate return. Extra copies should be available at the workshop for signing by applicants who failed to return theirs or by other attendees who are "admitted" at the last moment and for whom this serves as the only statement of voluntary participation.

Moderate Risk. This includes applicants of either sex who are 35 years or older, have no disability, and are free of overfat or health problems. Some in this group will have been physically active during recent years or months and, if impressively so, may be treated as low-risk applicants. Where doubt exists, it is justifiable to place them in the moderate-risk group, because of their age. This group also contains applicants younger than 35 who could not qualify for the low-risk group. These are people who are overly fat, who have health or disability problems, or those who are okay by these standards but have participated in little or no physical activity during recent months or years. In keeping with American College of Sports Medicine recommendations (16), people in this group should provide a statement from a medical practitioner that they have had a general, physical examination during the past six months and have been judged to be capable of participating in vigorous, physical activity without undue risk to their personal health. It would be ideal if the physical examination included a graded exercise stress test with ECG to voluntary exhaustion or, as minimal service, a submaximal work or resting ECG. Since, at the time of this writing, this may not be a realistic requirement for voluntary participation in exercise workshops, it may better serve as a recommendation that might sensitize both the applicant and the applicant's physician to its probable importance. In addition to the physician's statement, applicants in the moderate-risk group should sign a disclaimer statement of voluntary participation, as with the low-risk group. Since some applicants of the same age will be asked to provide a physician's statement while others will not, and since this might cause some unnecessary confusion, it can best be handled by treating the matter openly. When an applicant is requested to return a physician's statement (or, less ideally, bring one to present at the first session), the reason for the request should be clearly stated, for example, in view of the relatively long period since you have been physically active, because you have surpassed your 35th birthday, since you exceed our arbitrary weight relative to height standards (considerably less offensive than saying someone is overweight, overfat, or obese), because of your previous history of low-back pain and spinal problems, high blood pressure, and heart condition, we are requesting that you provide a physician's statement indicating that you are capable of participating in vigorous, physical activity without undue risk to your health. In addition to providing some basic protection to the exercise leader, requesting a physical examination can greatly benefit the applicant. If the physician is being asked to "clear" the patient for participation in vigorous physical activity he or she will carefully evaluate the normality of cardiovascular and lung function as well as any compromised neuromuscular or joint performance. Additionally, both parties will most likely reflect on the current status of the patient's general health, physical fitness, and normality of body weight. The physician will frequently recommend body weight reduction and increased physical activity and thereby becomes an important ally in the process of restoring the patient to a life of vigorous health and well-being. In cases where the physician's statement does not give total clearance to a patient, that is, clearance is given but only partially or conditionally, it would be advisable to consider these applicants as high-risk participants subject to the same special considerations as described below. Moderate-risk applicants who provide full clearance statements from physicians would not receive any special consideration and, for all practical purposes, would be treated as the low-risk participants during exercise sessions.

High Risk. This group includes those applicants of either sex who are 35 years or older and whose application responses were such that they could not reasonably be placed in the moderate-risk grouping. This group also includes those from the moderate-risk category who could not obtain a complete clearance statement from their examining physician. It is recommended that these high-risk applicants be required to submit a physician's statement and sign a voluntary participation statement as previously described but that they also be given some special considerations. First, it would not be unreasonable to refuse final acceptance of applicants who had previously been categorized as moderate- or high-risk individuals if they could not obtain a clearance statement from a physician (*Note.* all clearance statements should be retained along with each individual's application and signed voluntary participant statement). Second, even if they receive a complete clearance statement, it would be reasonable to hold a brief, private group conference with these applicants prior to beginning the workshop. During this conference, they should first be informed in a nonpersonal, group-address manner why they have been selected from the group-at-large. For example, because of their inability to obtain full clearance from their physician, because of their relative inactivity during the past several months, because of arbitrarily imposed standards by the workshop staff, or because of their previous health histories. They can then be verbally precautioned against attempting to exercise too vigorously, attempting to perform the exercises in the exact manner demonstrated (modification in form is usually also effective and allows time for adaptation), or keeping up with the group during exercise sessions. They should be told to work only within their own subjective performance limits and discontinue an activity or slow up if they feel unduly stressed at any time. It should be fully emphasized that it takes a considerable period of time to fully adapt to a life that includes vigorous physical activity, along with forewarnings that residual muscle and joint pains are inevitable.

Finally, the matter of individual variations in abilities, work capacities, and adaptation responsiveness should be mentioned and the importance of involvement and progression as an "individual" should be emphasized. This will tend to remove some of the competitiveness and ego drives that are nearly always present when people participate in group exercise activities. Many of these same remarks can be made to the other subgroups or the entire workshop group but, importantly, must be made to the high-risk group. The matter could, of course, be handled in a variety of ways other than speaking to them as a separate group. For example, if more than one exercise leader is available, they could each address a subgroup with the content of the address being somewhat different for each group. Using this approach, it would seem reasonable to advise all groups to avoid overexertion and modify or discontinue activities as needed. This would tend to neutralize the stigma attached to precautioning only the high-risk group if several people in this group begin to voluntarily drop out. A third approach would be to address the entire group, informing them of some of the hazards of overexertion during these beginning workouts, encouraging everyone to participate as individuals, and then expressing a special word of precaution to those individuals in the group who, for a variety of reasons, have not received full clearance to participate. Although this latter approach has some pitfalls—others wonder which participants have not received full clearance and why, and some who have not been cleared will work extra hard to avoid this identity—it may be the only practical one if only one workshop leader is involved. If this latter approach is used, those individuals regarded as being in the high-risk group should be informed of their conditional participation status (less alarming and more acceptable terms than high risk) in some private manner. A special note in their workshop packet, or a status designation on a standard form that each participant receives would be appropriate. In any case, avoid identifying such persons any more than necessary, while clearly stating the reason for their being categorized as conditional participants. Then when statements are made to the group that should have special relevance to them, they will clearly make the associated self-identification. A last, special consideration that can be given to the high-risk (conditional status) participants is to, as much as possible, observe them closely during exercise sessions, and continually encourage them to progress only as rapidly as their physiology will allow, that is, don't push too hard. Table 1 outlines the criterion for assigning participants to low-, moderate-, and high-risk categories and may be helpful once the overall concept contained in this chapter has been reviewed.

ADMINISTERING WORK TESTS   An additional method commonly used to acquire more information about the work tolerance of people attending workshops is to administer some form of initial work test. There are three advantages of having participants perform initial evaluation tests: (1) participants are immediately sensitized to the status of their strength or fitness, (2) weaknesses are identified, and (3) initial measurements have been made so that progress can be charted. Disadvantages to some tests are that they either do not identify weaknesses or are so strenuous that they produce undue soreness and may be unsafe to administer to generalized groups, especially when the health and fitness status of individuals in the group is entirely unknown. Many of these latter problems, however, can be circumvented by intelligent planning.

The work evaluation tests need not be complicated in either administration or interpretation. Basically, they fall into three categories: (1) those intended to evaluate the strength and endurance of localized muscle groups; (2) those for evaluating submaximal cardiovascular responses during exercise and recovery; and (3) those used to evaluate maximal cardiorespiratory or aerobic fitness. An example of each category of test will be given below along with some administrative tips.

TESTS OF LOCAL MUSCLE STRENGTH AND ENDURANCE These tests are easy to administer and should be given if any tests at all are used. Score sheets should be provided so that participants can quickly evaluate and record their performance on each item. Participants should be generally warmed up before they attempt the test items. They should do the items in the order given to avoid residual, localized fatigue that would dampen subsequent performances. The pass-fail standards are strictly arbitrary and may be easily met by many participants, while providing an "unnrealistic" and seemingly unattainable goal for others. It should be pointed out that the standards have been arbitrarily set but represent attainable, minimal performance goals that all skiers should be able to attain with proper exercises and training. Don't dwell on this too much and simply get

TABLE 1. Criterion for assigning applicants to low-, medium-, and high-exercise risk groups (see text for details)

GROUP	AGE	SEX	HEIGHT/WEIGHT	HEALTH STATUS	RECENT PHYSICAL ACTIVITY	ADDED REQUIREMENTS	STATUS DESIGNATIONS	SPECIAL CONSIDERATIONS
low	< 35 years	Either	Normal	Clear	Considerable	Disclaimer statement	Non-conditional	None
	Note. If any risk "signals" present, assign to moderate risk group!							
Moderate	< 35 years	Either	"Signal" risks—assigned from low group			Disclaimer and unqualified clearance from physician	Non-conditional	None
	> 35 years	Either	Normal	Clear	If considerable	Disclaimer statement	Non-conditional	None
	Note. If any "signals" present or only qualified clearance, assign to high risk group!							
High	> 35 years	Either	"Signal" risks—assigned from moderate group			Disclaimer statement and physician clearance—may be full or partial	Conditional	Individual identification,
	< 35 years	Either	"Signal" risks and only qualified clearance					Counseling on precautions, closely monitor

on with the tests, since they usually stimulate considerable interest and provide much important nonverbal feedback to the performer. The test items described below were selected because they measure strength and endurance of muscle groups of primary importance in skiing. This is consistent with the recommended procedural step of evaluating individual weaknesses in the section on optimal training. Other tests could be substituted for those given but they should meet criteria of being validly related to skiing, and they should have reasonable standards set for male and female performers.

Partial Squat Test. Measures the ability to sustain a partially flexed leg position while fully supporting body weight — a test of isometric strength and endurance of thigh muscles. Assume a standing bent-leg position as shown in Exercise 12B, but with arms fully extended forward, straight from the shoulders. Hold this postiion as long as tolerable or for one and one-half minutes. One must be able to hold steady for 45 seconds to pass this test. If done in pairs, the assistant times and records.

Push-Up Test. Measures arm and shoulder strength and endurance. Men do regular version from toes while women do modified version from knees. Record number that are correctly and continuously done allowing rest only in the up (weight supported) position. Must do 15 to pass. If done in pairs, the assistant judges, counts, and records.

Sit-Up Test. Measures strength and endurance of abdominal muscles. Assume back-lying, knees-bent position with hands interlaced behind head as shown in Exercise 1A. Assistant should hold feet down or place them under a heavy restrainer (bleacher supports, bench, etc.). Sit up, bringing elbows forward and in to touch knees and return. Do as many as possible in a 60-second period. Must do a minimum of 25 to pass this test. If done in pairs, the assistant holds the feet, judges, counts, and records.

Seated Stretch-Reach Test. Measures flexibility and extensibility of hamstring, back, and shoulder muscles and range of motion in associated joints. Assume seated, legs-together with straight-knees position as seen in Exercise 26B. Keeping knees down, stretch forward as far as possible with fingers toward or between large toes. Note position of finger tips in approximate one-inch units from toes (-5 in., -4 in., -3 in., -2 in., -1 in.), touching toes (0), or distance beyond toes (+1 in., +2 in., +3 in.). Must be able to stretch within three inches (approximately the length of little finger for men, ring finger for women) of toes to pass this test. If done in pairs, the assistant checks knee-down position, estimates distance, and records.

Leg Raise Test. Tests strength and endurance of abductors of thigh and gives indication of status of thigh adductors and rotators. Assume side-lying position as shown in Exercise 19B. Raise leg upward as far as possible, and return to start position. Repeat, doing as many as possible in 30 seconds, roll immediately to other side, and do as many as possible for the remainder of one minute. Record total amount done. Must do a minimum of 30 to pass. If done in pairs, the assistant times, counts, and records.

Newspaper Jump Test. Measures agility and strength and endurance of legs during vigorous, explosive-dynamic movements. Essentially the same as the box-jumping Exercise number 13, but use a section of newspaper folded in the standard, new-off-the-stand (two-way fold) manner. The performer starts with both feet on one side of the paper, hands on hips, and jumps the width of the paper, landing on both feet. Repeat, without touching the paper, as many times as possible in 60 seconds. Must complete 40 "good" jumps in 60 seconds to pass the test. If done in pairs, assistant judges, counts, and records completed jumps. If performers lose their jumping rhythm or co-ordination or feel overly stressed, they will usually do better by pausing to rest or to regain their balance and then begin again. For experience, count the pulse rate for the first 20 seconds after the person stops jumping, multiply by 3 and record this value. Generally, more physically fit people will have lower heart rates.

Figure 7 below outlines the recommended muscular strength and endurance test items and could be used as a guide to preparing score sheets or cards for use during the administration of the tests. In keeping with the previous discussion, it is prudent to caution participants against overexerting themselves during the performance of these test items. It is expected that some will fail to meet the arbitrarily defined minimal standards. It might be emphasized that their poor performance represents a valid reason for their having chosen to attend the workshop, that is, to determine how fit or unfit they currently are and then proceed to learn what best to do about it. Once again. competition between individuals should be played down, with emphasis placed on individual evaluation and performance. This can sometimes be partially accomplished by splitting up competitive groups or pairs

PHYSICAL PERFORMANCE SCORECARD
SKI-CONDITIONING WORKSHOP
Sponsor — Mt. Holly National Ski Patrol

Name _____   Date _____

Sex _____   Age _____   Years of ski experience _____

Ski competence level (x one) _____ Begin _____ Intermediate _____ Advanced

Physical fitness level (x one) _____ Low _____ Average _____ High

Scorers name _____   Application conditional _____ Unconditional _____

TEST ITEM	SCORE	MINIMAL PASS SCORE	ENTER PASS = P FAIL = F	TABLES
1. Partial squat (max 90 sec)	____ sec	45		A. Step test HR males 75– 80 Excellent 85– 90 Good 95–115 Average 120–125 Fair 130–135 Poor
2. Pushups (maximum	____ no.	15		
3. Situps (60 sec)	____ no.	25		B. Step test HR females 85– 90 Excellent

4. Stretch-
   reach   ——— in.   −3
   (−, 0, + in.)

5. Leg raise   ——— no.   30
   (60 sec)

6. Newspaper   ——— no.   40
   jump
   (60 sec)

7. Heart rate after newspaper jump ——— b/min.

8. Heart rate before stepping test ——— b/min.

9. Heart rate after stepping test ——— b/min.

10. Estimation of CV fitness from step test HR and Table A (males) or B (females) ——————— .

11. Distance run in 12 min ——————— miles to nearest 0.1 mile.

12. Estimation of "aerobics" fitness from distance run and Table C (males) or D (females) above ——————— .

                                               95–100 Good
    105–125 Average
    130–135 Fair
    140–145 Poor

C. 12-Min run – Males

D. 12-Min run – Females

   Note. See Figure 8 for
   these age and sex re-
   lated tables.

FIGURE 7. Example physical performance test score card.

by a purposeful assignment of partners and wise location of performers, that is, keep certain people separated. Furthermore, they can all be told that their personal performances are for their own knowledge and are not to be broadcast unless they wish to do so. Also they might be told that comparisons of scores will be made only after all persons have completed all test items, scores have been recorded, and all score cards returned to their owners. In most cases, the workshop staff will want to develop a system for duplicate record keeping so that participants can retain their personal performance score cards. This can be handled efficiently in a variety of ways, for example, carbon copies, Xerox copies made, or compilation of individual performances onto a master data sheet by each performer or a staff person. However handled, these data should be reviewed with each workshop attendee to identify unusual weaknesses where special efforts will yield great dividends. Data from the entire workshop group should also be reviewed to indicate how the participants performed as a whole, that is, how well individual performances related to each individual's own fitness perceptions as indicated on the workshop application and whether the arbitrary pass-fail standards need to be adjusted for subsequent workshop groups. These data, if used fully and properly, are an invaluable spin-off from the workshop itself.

Heart-Rate Recovery Test. The theoretical basis for these tests of cardiovascular response to submaximal work is that the amount of increase in heart rate during work and the rapidity of recovery following work are directly related to the general physical fitness of the individual, that is, for a given work task, the heart rate of a fit person does not go as high and recovers faster than that of an unfit person. Importantly, large increases in heart rate can also be related to excessive body fat or to muscles that are weak relative to the load (body weight) being raised and lowered. The most practical test to administer during a ski workshop is one devised by Kasch (17). It is a submaximal stepping test in which recovery heart rate is counted after participants step up and down on a bench approximately 12 inches high. In many cases, the bottom row of bleachers in a gymnasium can be effectively used for this purpose if the height is about 12 inches. The test can be administered to several people at the same time if participants are first paired and taught to count pulse rates by feeling at the wrist (just to the inside of top when hand is in hand-shake position) or at the neck (carotid artery or either side of the voice box and press in). Performers then step up and down on the bench at a cadence of 24 step-cycles per minute for three minutes. The proper cadence can be given by a metronome or called by a trained supervisor as "up-up-down-down." These verbal commands could, of course, be easily placed on recording tape for replay. At completion, the heart rate is counted during the first full minute of recovery with the subject seated and quiet. It is important that the count be started immediately after work is stopped, since recovery can be very fast, especially in well-trained persons. Subject B counts Subject A's recovery HR, records it, and their roles are reversed. Tables A and B in Figure 7 can be used to provide an approximate indication of each performer's cardiovascular fitness. Table A is for males and is based on many test results (17), while Table B is an extrapolated table for females based on known differences in resting and exercise heart rates between the sexes. It should be kept in mind that the application of these tables does not necessarily provide a "perfect" indication of the fitness status of all individuals but instead provides a general indication utilizing broad categories.

Tests of Maximal Cardiorespiratory (Aerobic) Fitness. Although several tests of cardiorespiratory fitness have been promoted, the best test to give to a workshop group is the 12-minute run for distance as described by Cooper (16). This field test is easy to administer to groups, does not require special equipment, can be conducted in a variety of settings, and is relatively safe if all applicants are screened as previously indicated. The test can be run on a track, on paved streets, or open fields or roads with the main criterion being that the terrain is flat. A massed start can usually be used, and a signal can be given to indicate the end of 12 minutes. Runners must, of course, be within hearing limits of the stop signal. If approximate distances have been previously marked off, it is very easy for one scorer to record for the entire group. The runners should be told to continue to run in place during recovery until their distances have been recorded. This will reduce some of the light-headedness and feelings of faintness common in persons who are unaccustomed to running. Participants should also be told to sit or lie down if they feel extremely faint and that this action will serve as a request for aid. Another approach is to have runners remember where they stopped on the tracks, then walk back to the start for a desirable recovery. Distances can be measured and recorded thereafter.

Some participants will not be able to run continuously for 12 minutes and should walk until they can resume a faster pace. They should be precautioned about starting too fast, which can produce such effects as early, local fatigue, general exhaustion, or stitch-in-the-side. They should be told that a steady pace usually produces best results and that, if they want to run harder, to do so in the final minutes. They should also be told that they do not have to take the test and that they should discontinue running if they experience undue chest pain or muscle "pulls."

Tables for interpreting the results of the 12-minute run for distance are shown in Figure 8. These tables are based on run tests administered to large numbers of subjects and are included through courtesy of Dr. Ken Cooper, Founder and Director of the Aerobics Institute, Dallas, Texas. They are based on both age and sex and, as for the step test tables, provide a general indication of the level of a performer's cardiorespiratory or aerobic fitness. Note that the fitness categories are based on distance run, and that there exists a range of distance for each category. In reality, this makes scoring an easy matter, since the scorer only needs to note into which range each performer falls rather than attempting to record the exact distance run in miles and yards. However, accurate records should be kept for future progress checks for each individual.

The results of the strength tests, step test and 12-minute run coupled with the application information now provide a good profile of each workshop applicant. While this information is useful to the workshop staff and allows them to provide a much better service, the measures are also usually extremely enlightening to the participant. For some, it will be the first time in many years that any quantifiable measures have been made of their work capabilities and physiological responses. Nearly all will be keenly sensitized to the status, be it good, bad or somewhere between, of their physical fitness. For many, this can serve as a very real stimulus to "shock" them into action that lasts for a long period. For others, the effect will only be short term and, in a few cases, the response will be continued and accepted apathy. In these latter cases, it is interesting to note that the effects are often not immediately apparent but are experienced as delayed changes in physical activity and healthful living behavior.

A final word of caution concerning interpretation and inferences about a participant's general health seems appropriate. It would be

TABLE C. Twelve-minute test for men
(distances in miles covered in 12 minutes)

FITNESS CATEGORY	AGE			
	UNDER 30	**30–39**	**40–49**	**50+**
I. Very poor	<1.0	<.95	<.85	<.80
II. Poor	1.00-1.24	.95-1.14	.85-1.04	.80- .99
III. Fair	1.25-1.49	1.15-1.39	1.05-1.29	1.00-1.24
IV. Good	1.50-1.74	1.40-1.64	1.30-1.54	1.25-1.49
V. Excellent	1.75+	1.65+	1.55+	1.50+

<Means less than.

TABLE D. Twelve-minute test for women*
(distance in miles covered in 12 minutes)

FITNESS CATEGORY	AGE			
	UNDER 30	**30–39**	**40–49**	**50+**
I. Very poor	<.95	<.85	<.75	<.65
II. Poor	.95-1.14	.85-1.04	.75- .94	.65- .84
III. Fair	1.15-1.34	1.05-1.24	.95-1.14	.85-1.04
IV. Good	1.35-1.64	1.25-1.54	1.15-1.44	1.05-1.34
V. Excellent	1.65+	1.55+	1.45+	1.35+

*Preliminary chart based on limited data.
<Means less than.

FIGURE 8. Tables C (men) and D (women) for determining fitness category from distance run during 12-minute test. (From *The New Aerobics* by Kenneth H. Cooper, M.D. Copyright © 1970 by Kenneth H. Cooper. Reprinted by permission of the publisher, M. Evans and Company, New York, N.Y., 10017.)

entirely unwarranted to assume, for example, that an HR recovery value of 150 beats per/minute following the step test indicates a diseased state of the heart or cardiovascular system. Such an interpretation would be entirely inappropriate and out of the jurisdiction of workshop staff. If these results occur, it is usually best to check to be sure that no errors in measurement have been made, that is, the step test could be rerun after a few minutes recovery with nearly the same response. If measurements are correct and participants display undue anxiety over the results, it would then be appropriate to suggest that they have them reviewed by their family physician.

ORGANIZATIONAL METHODS

Training workshops can take a variety of forms depending on, for example, the group size, whether they're set up as single versus multiple sessions, or as demonstrations versus participation workshops. Our objective here is to describe some common methods of organizing workshops, a review that might prove useful to committees and individuals as they design workshops to best meet local needs.

WORKSHOP SIZE AND NUMBER OF PARTICIPANTS One of the advantages of preregistration and setting an early deadline is that the organizers know quite accurately how many will be attending the workshop. This allows for selection of a room that is reasonable in size and also in rental cost, if that is a consideration. Professionals in show business know very well the importance of selecting facilities that are well-matched to the anticipated audience. A large space with few people is ineffective, and it is nearly as deadly as attempting to handle a large group in limited space. If possible, allow enough floor space so that if everyone participated simultaneously, there would be room for each person to lie spreadeagled without touching. This requires 30 to 36 square feet per participant. If it is impossible to reserve this much floor space, then alternatives to total group simultaneous participation must be explored. Application of the 30 to 36 square feet per participant rule is also limited by group size, since leadership effectiveness is diminished when the group size exceeds 40. When a single instructor teaches exercises to a group where all are actively participating, the number of participants should not exceed 40. An exception to this rule would be where a raised platform and sound amplification system is available for the leader. In such cases, the number of participants that might be effectively handled by a single leader could reasonably be increased to 100. If the number of participants exceeds 100, then alternative methods for handling large groups as described under single versus multiple leaders below should be employed.

In summary, we believe it is best if arrangements can be made for enough space to allow all participants to simultaneously engage in exercises with effective limits set at 40 and 100. This is not always possible, however, and leaders are frequently requested to conduct workshops in areas where the ratio of space per participant is inadequate. In these instances, the idea of total group simultaneous participation must be abandoned, since the needs for safe and effective individual participation do not change. A way out of this predicament is to set up circuit-training stations that require varying amounts of space (see section on circuit training below) or to devise presentation protocols where pairs of exercises are presented and then performed. One of the paired exercises would require maximum space for performance, while the second would require only minimum space. With this approach, all participants could be out on the floor at once but organized in alternating rows. Following a demonstration of each pair of exercises, rows 1, 3, and 5 would perform Exercise A (maximum space), while rows 2, 4, and 6 would perform Exercise B (minimum space), and then they would reverse their assignments. The success of this approach obviously resides in the leader's ability to organize a program of exercises that provides good balance between the space demands of the paired exercises.

SINGLE VERSUS MULTIPLE MEETING Training workshops may be conducted for a portion of a day or for two to three days. In some cases, the term workshop has been used to indicate a series of sessions held once or twice a week over several weeks, but we would prefer to call these sessions training or conditioning programs. In any case, the idea of the training workshop is to present the exercises and conditioning procedures in a manner in which they are properly understood and can be practiced by the participants while at home. The workshop is not intended to attempt to physically recondition the participants "overnight." On the contrary, most participants, because of their poor status of conditioning, would show a regression in physical-work performance if tested the day after they had vigorously exercised during a workshop session.

If only a single meeting is planned, then it is important to review and demonstrate all of the exercises, even if the participants have only a limited chance to practice them. A more relaxed approach could be used, of course, if more than one training workshop is planned as part of a comprehensive meeting. In cases where conditioning programs are organized, it is possible to use even a more gradual approach to presenting new exercises, since there is ample opportunity to learn and practice them on-the-spot. The quantity of written, audiovisual aid and other prepared support materials needed to conduct a successful workshop is somewhat inversely related to the number of sessions. Some ideas on these important matters are given later.

SINGLE VERSUS MULTIPLE LEADERS In instances where there exists a competent workshop staff, it is possible to organize the proceedings to utilize more than one exercise leader. This concept can also be applied where exceptionally large numbers (greater than 100) of participants have registered for the workshop which will be conducted in a large gymnasium or in separate rooms. It is desirable to use the multiple-leader approach whenever possible, since participants can identify more closely with a leader and can be supervised and monitored closely while learning and practicing the exercises. The multiple-leader approach should not be attempted, however, unless the staff is adequately prepared in advance, or additional time is allowed to coordinate efforts before the workshop begins. To do otherwise will result in chaos. The leader should assume nothing and be fully convinced that the group assistants are competently prepared to undertake the responsibility of subgroup leadership before assigning them to the task. In no case should the workshop leader breeze in a few minutes before the start of the workshop assuming that all assistants are schooled, assigned, and ready to proceed. The world just doesn't move in such a smooth manner!

Subgroup leaders can be used to good advantage in a variety of workshop settings. Even with smaller numbers of participants, they can be dispersed throughout the total group to answer questions or to constructively criticize and assist participants who are having difficulty in quickly learning to properly perform exercises. If the group is organized in this way, the exercise leader still retains responsibility for describing and demonstrating proper performance of each exercise. In cases where more than 100 have registered for the workshop, the use of multiple leaders is a must. If the exercise sessions are conducted in a large gymnasium, the role of the principal leader could remain the same as above, that is, he or she is responsible for describing and demonstrating each exercise prior to performance by subgroups. On the other hand, the principal leader could assume responsibilities of directing the organization of subgroups, reviewing selected exercises that are more troublesome to learn, and then turn the actual conduct of activities over to subgroup leaders who would follow a predetermined plan and time schedule. This latter approach is about the only reasonable way to organize a workshop with large numbers and separate rooms. The major organizational objective is to hold a meeting of the total group split into active-participation subgroups and then regroup at a fixed time. The importance of having a well-trained staff of subgroup-exercise leaders is readily apparent here.

DEMONSTRATION VERSUS PARTICIPATION Although ski conditioning exercises could be taught using a verbal description-demonstration approach, there is no substitute for first-hand, active participation. In this way, all participants "feel" the activities as well as see and hear about them. We strongly recommend that, whenever possible, workshops should be conducted on a participation basis. This has implications for the type of dress worn by the participants. They should be told to come dressed and ready to vigorously partici-pate in activities. It is usually wise to warn them that they will be doing exercises in a mixed group, in a variety of positions and set-tings, and that warm-up suits and slacks are more appropriate than skirts or loose-fitting shorts. Having them dressed when they arrive eliminates one clothes-changing crush that can be especially time-consuming, especially if dressing facilities are not available. Be sure to alert participants as to whether showers will be available for use and, if so, request that they bring their own towels. Even if shower and locker room facilities are available, participants should be re-quested to dress at home and pack their street clothes to avoid the initial rush. After the workshop is over, they can do as they please with regard to dressing and showering. During these times, a word of caution regarding the handling of valuables seems appropriate. This problem is partially solved if locks and lockers are available. Since this is frequently not the case, it is advisable to issue the usual standard warnings about carefully guarding personal valuables, but also provide envelopes for checking valuables to a responsible person. Simply use manila envelopes that are consecutively numbered on the back side with a large number in the center of the envelope and the same number in a tag partially cut from the adhesive flap. The tag is torn free and given to the checker as a future claim tag. The claim tags should be carried on the person and concientious efforts should be made to avoid losing them. The envelopes can be used repeated-ly if returned to a convenient depository in the shower or dressing area.

CIRCUIT-TRAINING METHOD Circuit training is an organizational approach that has been used to good advantage in weight-training classes where large numbers of students must frequently be handled with only limited equipment. In the organizational scheme, numbered, activity stations are set up in a circuit, splitting up the total group so that equal numbers are assigned to each station and having the subgroups rotate in order to the next station at a given signal. The transit time between stations should not be great or the location of each station confusing, since much of the effectiveness of the circuit is then lost, that is, it is not a good arrangement when separate rooms are used for the workshop. Likewise, the time needed for all people in each subgroup to complete the exercises "required" at each station should be similar. In this way, everyone will be active until the signal is given to move on to the next station. The exercises to be performed at each station should be staggered in terms of muscle groups worked, whether it is a stretching or strengthening activity, high versus low intensity, and individual versus buddy approach. If this is done, the participants will be able to complete the circuit without undue discomfort or fatigue.

Various combinations of demonstrations by principal leaders and utilization of exercise-station leaders are possible within the framework of the circuit-training approach. In some cases, it will work best to demonstrate several exercises in rapid succession, to have participation at each exercise station under the direction of station leaders, and then to regroup for the next series of demonstrations. During the second and subsequent series, the station leaders can remain at their same stations and simply assume responsibility for the next exercise they have been assigned. This usually works well, since each station leader can read up on their own exercises in advance and really become expert about them in terms of muscle groups, optimum training, and special needs for effectiveness, for example. Another approach using circuit-training procedures would be to have a general-orientation session including a demonstration of only difficult exercises and then begin the circuit. The station leaders would be responsible for demonstrating and teaching each exercise, for leading active participation, and for changing activities after each complete rotation of the circuit. Once again, this latter approach places more responsibility on station leaders and requires that they be more knowledgeable and better prepared.

MATERIAL AND EQUIPMENT NEEDS Conduction of the workshop can be greatly simplified if materials and equipment are prepared and obtained well in advance. It would be good to inform all participants that the workshop will be conducted following the general content of this book and to indicate where they might purchase a copy. Using the same names for exercises can do much to eliminate confusion during the activity sessions, and placards could be prepared for posting at exercise stations when the circuit-training approach is used. These placards can contain the station number, exercise name, and stickman drawing of the basic exercise positions involved. Another idea that works well is to prepare personal exercise sheets to be given to each person at the start of the workshop. These sheets should list the names of the exercises in the order presented, a corresponding stickman figure in the most descriptive exercise position, recommended number of repetitions or hold times, and a place for notations by the participant. This procedure reduces to a minimum the amount of such paraphernalia as notebooks, books, and clipboards that some participants may want to carry along during the activity sessions, and it aids greatly in the participant's retention of the supportive objectives and in proper execution of each exercise.

Finally, Table 2 contains a list of equipment, personnel, materials, and facility needs for conducting workshops. Most organizers will benefit by using it as a checklist to be sure that at least major considerations have been given some advance thought. After that, the amount of attention given to minor details and refinements is usually the distinguishing factor between a workshop that is judged to be outstanding rather than just good.

TABLE 2. Checklist of facilities, materials, personnel, and equipment needs for conducting ski-conditioning workshops.

FACILITIES

——————   Address of building _____

——————   Is it appropriately located? _____

——————   Name, position, address, and phone of contact person _____

                 _____

——————   Date of written request _____

——————   Date of written approval _____

——————   Cost of rental $_____ Rooms reserved _____

——————   Other rooms available _____

——————   Clean-up agreement _____

——————   Dressing rooms _____ Lockers _____

——————   Shower facilities _____

——————   Parking _____

——————   Building access _____

——————   Security and keys _____

——————   Emergency procedures _____

MATERIALS

——————   Announcements, date sent and posted _____

——————   Application forms

——————   Workshop program and schedule

——————   Envelopes for valuables

——————   Performance-test scorecards

——————   Workshop packets (pick up at registration)

——————   Nametags

TABLE 2. (continued)

_____ Exercise-station placards

_____ Individual exercise-notation sheets

_____ Slides or other AV materials

PERSONNEL

_____ Registration staff

_____ Exercise subgroup or station leaders

_____ Valuables—check-in

_____ Information desk

_____ First aid and emergency

_____ Audiovisual equipment

EQUIPMENT

_____ Pillows	_____ Sound amplification
_____ Beach balls	_____ First-aid kit
_____ 2 X 4 inch boards	_____ Stopwatch
_____ Ski poles	_____ Pencils
_____ Skis and boots	_____ Clipboards
_____ Slide projector	_____ Whistle
_____ Barbells	_____ Dumbbells
_____ Sand-bag weights	_____ Broomstick sections
_____ Newspapers	
_____ Benches	
_____ Rolled newspapers	
_____ Boxes	
_____ Mats	
_____ Ankle weights	

SECTION 9
References

1. Gwen Rector Robinson, *Skiing: Conditioning and Technique,* Mayfield Publishing Co., Palo Alto, California, 1974.

2. George Twardokens, *Skiing,* Goodyear Publishing Co., Pacific Palisades, California, 1971.

3. Georges Joubert and Jean Vuarnet, *How to Ski the New French Way,* The Dial Press, New York, 1967.

4. *Ski* (Incorporating: *Ski Life*), Universal Publishing and Distributing Corp., New York.

5. *Skiing,* Subscription Service Office, Flushing, New York.

6. A. E. Ellison, "Skiing injuries," (Editorial), *JAMA, 223,* 917 (1973).

7. G. L. Wilson, "The kinesiology and fraudulence of skiing," *Industrial Medicine and Surgery, 36,* 35–40 (1967).

8. Hans Kraus and Janet Nelson, "A Rebuilt You — Revolutionary Safety Device," *Ski, 37,* 72–75 (1972).

9. G. Agnevik and B. Saltin, *Utforsakning,* Idrottsfysiologi, Rapport nr 2.

10. F. B. Petersen et al., "The effect of varying the number of muscle contractions on dynamic muscle training," *Int. Z. angew, Physiol., 18,* 468 (1961).

11. J. W. Hansen, "The training effect of repeated isometric muscle contraction," *Int. Z. angew, Physiol., 18,* 474 (1961).

12. R. Berger, "Effect of Varied Weight Training Programs on Strength," *Research Quarterly of AAHPER, 33,* 168 (1962).

13. I. Astrand et al., "Intermittent muscular work," *Acta Physiol. Scand., 48,* 448 (1960).

14. W. Haddon, Jr., A. E. Ellison, and R. E. Carroll, "Skiing Injuries: Epidemiological Study," *Public Health Reports, 77,* 975-985 (1962).

15. K. Cooper, *The New Aerobics,* M. Evans and Company, New York, 1970.

16. American College of Sports Medicine, *Guidelines For Graded Exercise Testing and Exercise Prescription,* Lea and Febiger, 1975.

17. T. Pedersen, "Shape Up to Ski," *Skiing, 25,* 24-26 (October, 1972).

INDEX